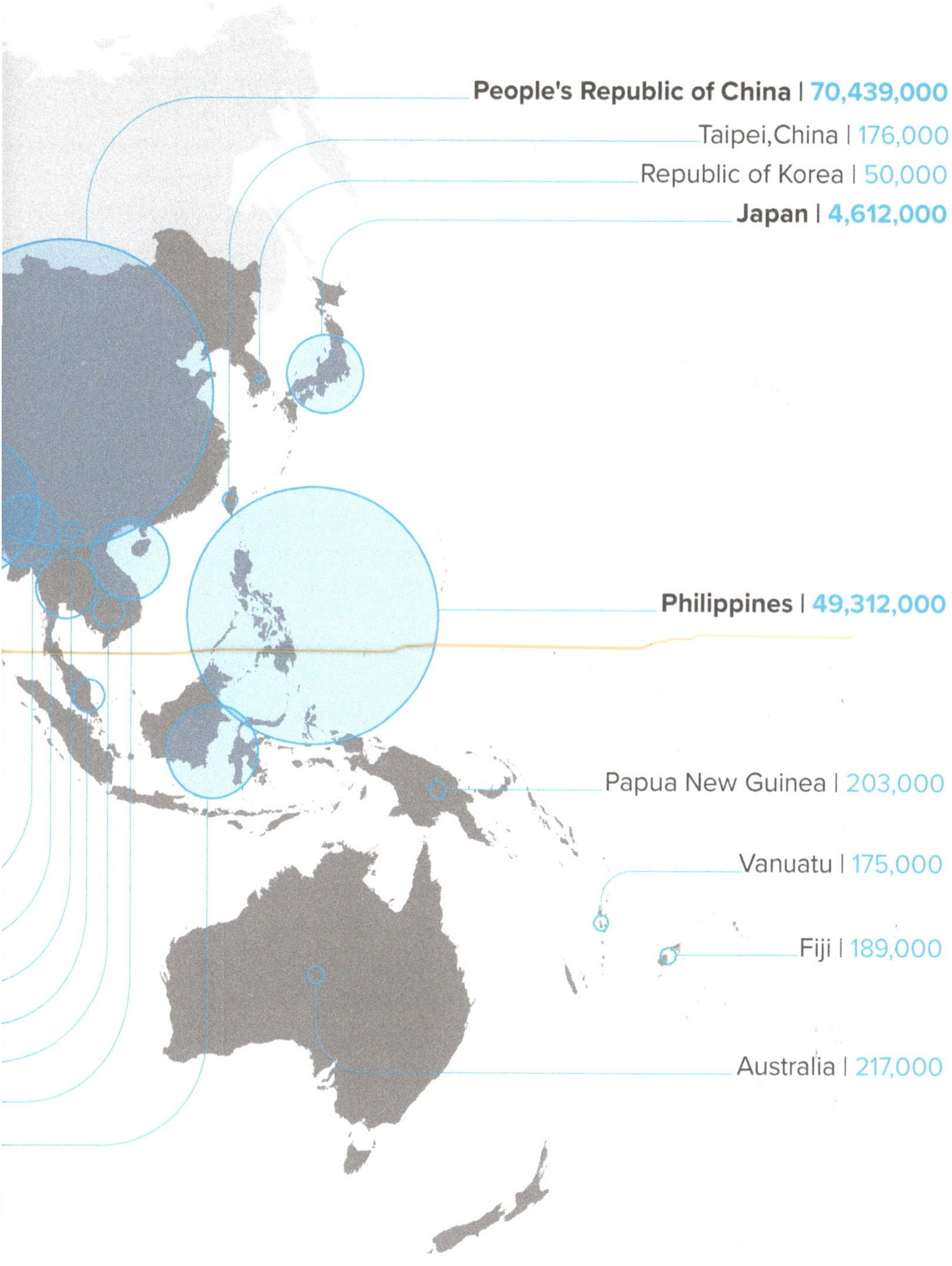

People's Republic of China | **70,439,000**

Taipei,China | 176,000

Republic of Korea | 50,000

Japan | **4,612,000**

Philippines | **49,312,000**

Papua New Guinea | 203,000

Vanuatu | 175,000

Fiji | 189,000

Australia | 217,000

17.9m **Central and West Asia** (8%)

914,000 **The Pacific** (0.4%)

The boundaries and the names shown on this map do not imply official endorsement or acceptance by IDMC.

Table of Contents

List of Figures and Boxes

Acknowledgements

ISBN 978-92-9269-728-0 (print); 978-92-9269-729-7 (electronic)

This report was financed by the Asian Development Bank (ADB) under the technical assistance project Understanding Disaster Displacement in Asia and the Pacific led by Steven Goldfinch. This publication has been funded in part by the Australian Government through the Department of Foreign Affairs and Trade. Additional thanks go to IDMC's core funding partners including the European Union, German Federal Foreign Office, German Federal Ministry for Economic Cooperation and Development, Liechtenstein's Ministry of Foreign Affairs, Norwegian Ministry of Foreign Affairs, Swedish International Development Cooperation Agency, and United States Agency for International Development.

Direction and project management: Alexandra Bilak, Bina Desai, and Christelle Cazabat

Project Coordination: Vicente Anzellini and Fanny Teppe

Drafting and Research: Vicente Anzellini, Christelle Cazabat, Pablo Cortés Ferrández, Ricardo Fal-Dutra Santos, Vincent Fung, Kathryn Giffin, Thannaletchimy Housset, Alesia O'Connor, Fanny Teppe, and Louisa Yasukawa

Data and Analysis: Sylvain Ponserre, Ghjulia Sialelli and Fanny Teppe

Design, layout, maps and graphs: Vivcie Bendo, Stéphane Kluser (Komplo), Emiliano Pérez, Sylvain Ponserre

Peer Review: We extend our thanks to the following reviewers: Gabriela Nataly Alvarez (IOM), Nina Birkeland (NRC), Steven Goldfinch (ADB), Rose McKenzie (ADB), Yanick Michaud-Marcotte (UNDRR-ROAP), Rebekah Ramsay (World Bank) and Yip Ching Yu (IOM).

Editor: Melanie Kelleher

Cover: Flood and erosion defense. A villager washes clothes on the banks of the river Brahmaputra in Assam, India. The Integrated Flood and Riverbank Erosion Risk Management Investment program, funded by ADB, has given people confidence to live and work in the area. Floods are among the primary hazards of concern and account for most weather-induced displacements. (Photo by Asian Development Bank)

Expansion in Thailand. Highway 12 from Phitsanulok to Lom Sak (105 km) is part of the Greater Mekong Subregion Highway Expansion Project in Thailand. (Photo by Asian Development Bank)

Abbreviations

ADB: Asian Development Bank

ADPC: Asian Disaster Preparedness Center

ASEAN: Association of Southeast Asian Nations

DRR: Disaster Risk Reduction

GDP: Gross Domestic Product

IDI: Internal Displacement Index

IDMC: Internal Displacement Monitoring Centre

IDP: Internally Displaced Person

IFRC: International Federation of Red Cross and Red Crescent Societies

IOM: International Organization for Migration

IPCC: Intergovernmental Panel on Climate Change

OCHA: United Nations Office for the Coordination of Humanitarian Affairs

PDD: Platform on Disaster Displacement

PRC: People's Republic of China

RCPs: Representative Concentration Pathways

SIDS: Small Island Developing States

UN: United Nations

UNDRR: United Nations Office for Disaster Risk Reduction

UNGA: United Nations General Assembly

UNHCR: United Nations High Commissioner for Refugees

UNICEF: United Nations Children's Fund

WMO: World Meteorological Organization

Currency Equivalents

(as of 30 June 2022)

Currency unit – Nepalese rupees (NRs)
NR1.00 = $0.0079
$1.00 = NRs126.17

Currency unit – Papua New Guinea kina (K)
K1.00 = $0.28
$1.00 = K3.57

Currency unit – Indonesian rupiah (Rp)
Rp1.00 = $0.000067
$1.00 = Rp14,937.65

Foreword

Globally, Asia and the Pacific is the region most affected by disaster displacement. Each year, the lives of millions of people are disrupted by disasters. While disasters and displacement are not new to the region, the scale of displacement is increasing. The impacts from events are compounded by climate change and other drivers of risk, including rapid and sometimes unregulated urbanization, as well as economic vulnerability and fragility, which result in recurring and protracted displacement.

The figures are sobering. Largely triggered by weather-related hazards, a total of 225.3 million internal displacements were reported in Asia and the Pacific during the period 2010–2021. This represents an annual average of 18.8 million—or around 78%—of the global total disaster displacement during this period.

While displacement often demands a humanitarian response, it is first and foremost a development issue. It disrupts and erodes the development gains of affected communities and can have an impact on their longer-term stability and resilience to future shocks. Reducing displacement risk and providing solutions to those affected by displacement requires that decisions and investments are risk-informed, drawing from an evidence base that recognizes the complexities that countries and communities now face.

A 2021 report of the United Nations Secretary-General's High-Level Panel on Internal Displacement calls for fundamental changes to the current approach to solutions. The panel's overall message was clear: more of the same is not good enough. This includes addressing the drivers of displacement, reducing displacement risk and strengthening the effective use of internal displacement data.

The Asian Development Bank (ADB) and the Internal Displacement Monitoring Centre (IDMC) have published this report to contribute to this agenda, by providing the latest evidence on the scale and impacts of disaster displacement in the region and supporting actions for durable solutions in the prevention, response, and recovery. The report represents a reference to governments and stakeholders to inform policy measures and practical actions that can be taken to prevent, reduce, and better manage displacement risk.

Disaster displacement is a significant challenge for the region that, unless addressed, is set to increase. However, there are opportunities to meet this challenge, including through scaling-up efforts to strengthen community resilience, and the explicit inclusion of displacement in urban planning, risk governance, and social protection, to name just a few.

ADB is committed to achieving a prosperous, inclusive, resilient, and sustainable Asia and the Pacific. Addressing displacement risk and its drivers will be critical for the region to meet its sustainable development ambitions and efforts to scale-up support to ADB developing member countries to strengthen their resilience to climate change and natural hazards.

Noelle O'Brien
Chief of Climate Change and Disaster Risk Management Thematic Group concurrently Director
Asian Development Bank

Alexandra Bilak
Director
Internal Displacement Monitoring Centre

Fiji's natural hazards. While the Pacific Island of Fiji is picturesque, IDMC estimates that around 5,800 people on average are likely to be displaced during any given year by hazards such as earthquakes, tsunamis, cyclonic winds and storm surges. (Photo by Asian Development Bank)

Key Messages

1

Asia and the Pacific is the region most affected by disaster displacement worldwide.

2

The cost of disasters in the region is estimated to be several hundred billions of dollars each year. This does not include the economic impact of displacement itself.

3

Climate change—combined with the rapid urbanization of the region and other factors—may significantly heighten future displacement risk and related costs.

4

Investment in the prevention of disaster displacement is the only sustainable course of action for the socioeconomic development of the region.

5

The region already has successful initiatives to prevent, monitor, respond to, and end disaster displacement that can inform future action.

Key Findings

1

There were over 225 million internal displacements—or movements—in Asia and the Pacific during 2010–2021, which was over three-quarters of the global total for this period.

2

East Asia and Southeast Asia had the highest number of disaster displacements—nearly two-thirds of the total—closely followed by South Asia. All three subregions are densely populated and highly exposed to various hazards. Pacific island states bear the greatest displacement risk relative to their population size.

3

Weather-related hazards—such as monsoon rains and tropical storms—were responsible for 95% of all disaster displacements across the region during 2010–2021.

4

Financial costs and losses weigh disproportionately on those with limited resources. Each time a person is displaced, costs arise. Economic impacts add up when displaced people are uprooted for months, years, or even decades.

5

Investment in sustainable development and taking early action to address internal displacement will be more effective and less costly than relying on humanitarian aid in the long term. Robust data on the scale, duration, and severity of disaster displacement —as well as its impacts on people and economies—will help guide actions to mitigate the negative consequences and seize potential opportunities for risk reduction and solutions.

6

There has been significant progress across the region to develop disaster displacement policies and translate words into action. Much still remains to be done to effectively mitigate the impact of disaster displacement on individuals, societies, and economies.

Risk of cyclones in Tonga. IDMC estimates that there is a 64% probability that, in the next 50 years, around 21,400 people will be displaced as a result of cyclonic winds in the Pacific archipelago. (Photo by Asian Development Bank)

Introduction

Most of the disaster displacement recorded globally has taken place in the Asia and Pacific region. An estimated 225.3 million internal displacements—or forced movements—were recorded during 2010–2021. Large-scale storms and floods, droughts, earthquakes, tsunamis, and volcanic eruptions keep displacing millions of people every year across this vast region that is home to most of the world's population.

Medium- to small-scale disasters also put a toll on the resilience of communities and countries to shocks, and the impacts of displacement vary significantly across geographies and economies. Low- and middle-income countries and small island states face specific challenges in preventing and responding to disaster displacement, which will require tailored approaches to confront the challenges posed by the compounding impacts of poverty and inequality, unsustainable urbanization, land degradation and erosion, and climate change, to only name a few.

Many gaps in understanding the full scale and scope of displacement persist. This includes the number of people who remain displaced after disasters and the duration of their displacement. In addition, few assessments allow an understanding of the indirect and long-term social and economic impacts of displacement in the context of disasters, which hampers the design and implementation of sound policies for durable solutions and risk reduction.

This report aims to fill some of these gaps. It presents the disaster displacement trends in the region during 2010–2021 and provides insights into its social and economic impacts. The report also discusses the opportunities ahead, by highlighting the progress made across the region in preventing and responding to disaster displacement. It aims to serve as a basis to raise awareness of this phenomenon, encourage further investments in risk reduction and durable solutions, and guide policy toward this end.

The report is structured in four chapters. Part 1 looks at disaster displacement trends during 2010–2021. It analyzes the main hazards triggering displacement and provides a subregional breakdown presenting the main drivers and impacts of disaster displacement across geographies.

Part 2 discusses the social and economic impacts of displacement in the region and analyzes results from research in selected countries. Part 3 unpacks several dimensions of the phenomenon, including the types of displacement across the disaster risk management cycle, the seasonal nature of the phenomenon, and the role of climate change.

Part 4 discusses the policy landscape as of 2021 to prevent and prepare for disaster displacement in Asia and the Pacific, and the role that the Sendai Framework for Disaster Risk Reduction will have in galvanizing action for risk reduction and prevention.

Definitions, Methodological Considerations, and Caveats

When looking at the data presented in this report, some methodological issues and caveats influencing the trends should be considered.

Data collection on disaster damages and losses has increased significantly across the region. For this reason, displacement trends may seem to be stable or even increasing in some countries and subregions, but the availability of data may play a role.

Some displacements reported since 2010 have been in the form of pre-emptive evacuations organized by governments, which is a testimony to the increased risk awareness and enhanced disaster risk management in several countries. This is a reminder that displacement is not always a negative outcome but can save lives, and in some contexts can be an effective resilience measure. Very few countries in the region differentiate pre-emptive movements from those happening during or after disasters. Disaggregating such data is therefore impossible. For this reason, displacements happening before, during, and after disasters are presented under the metric "internal displacements".

The availability of data and population sizes vary significantly across the region, which also influences the overall trends. Displacement figures should therefore be looked at with caution and considered relative to a country's population and its capacity to monitor, reduce, and address disaster displacement.

This report uses the following metrics and definitions:

Internal displacements (also referred to as disaster displacements) correspond to the estimated number of forced movements of people within the borders of their country caused by disasters. Pre-emptive movements are also counted under this metric, but it is not possible to disaggregate by pre- and post-disaster displacement due to lack of data.

Figures include individuals who have been displaced more than once. In this sense, the number of internal displacements does not equal the number of people displaced during the year. Although it would be fair to assume that a high number of internal displacements is linked to high population exposure—as would be the case in highly populated countries like India or the People's Republic of China (PRC)—the number of disaster displacements cannot be looked at relative to the population of a country. For example, in the event of two large-scale cyclones hitting the same area in a year, people may be forced to move twice, and their movements would be counted as such. If this data is looked at relative to the area population, it would lead to incorrect results.

The total number of internally displaced people (IDPs) corresponds to the total number of people living in internal displacement as of 31 December 2021. Given the lack of data on this metric, most of the data presented in this report use internal displacements instead of the total number of IDPs.

Protracted displacement refers to a situation in which the process of securing a durable solution to displacement is stalled, and/or internally displaced people are marginalized as a consequence of a lack of protection of their human rights.[1]

Part 1

Internal Displacement Trends in Asia and the Pacific (2010–2021)

Sustainable Tourism Development. Investing in environmentally sustainable activities at the local level can mitigate the risk of displacement linked with climate change and lack of livelihood opportunities. (Photo by Asian Development Bank)

The Asia and Pacific region accounts for the majority of global disaster displacement, with 225.3 million internal displacements reported during 2010–2021 (Figure 2). This represents an annual average of 18.8 million and is equivalent to around 78% of the global total during this period. Displacement impacts vary significantly across this vast region, which contains highly populated countries such as India, the People's Republic of China (PRC), and the Philippines, as well as highly exposed small island states and territories such as Fiji, Tuvalu, and Vanuatu.

The region has a long history of devastating disasters that marked entire generations, and although internal displacement has been a reality for centuries, it is not until recently that the true scale has started to become apparent. The Internal Displacement Monitoring Centre (IDMC) has been recording disaster displacement globally since 2008, but for this report, the data covers the timeframe 2010–2021.[2]

This chapter presents the hazards triggering disaster displacement in the region and provides a more in-depth look at the specificities of the five subregions: East Asia, Southeast Asia, South Asia, Central and West Asia, and the Pacific.[3] The analysis of these displacement trends constitutes an important evidence base for strengthening disaster risk reduction and durable solutions efforts in a region that is challenged by current and emerging risks associated with urbanization, land degradation, erosion, and the impacts of climate change. The historical perspective presented in this section also offers insights into the need for governments, United Nations organizations, civil society organizations, and communities to invest in measures to reduce disaster displacement risk.

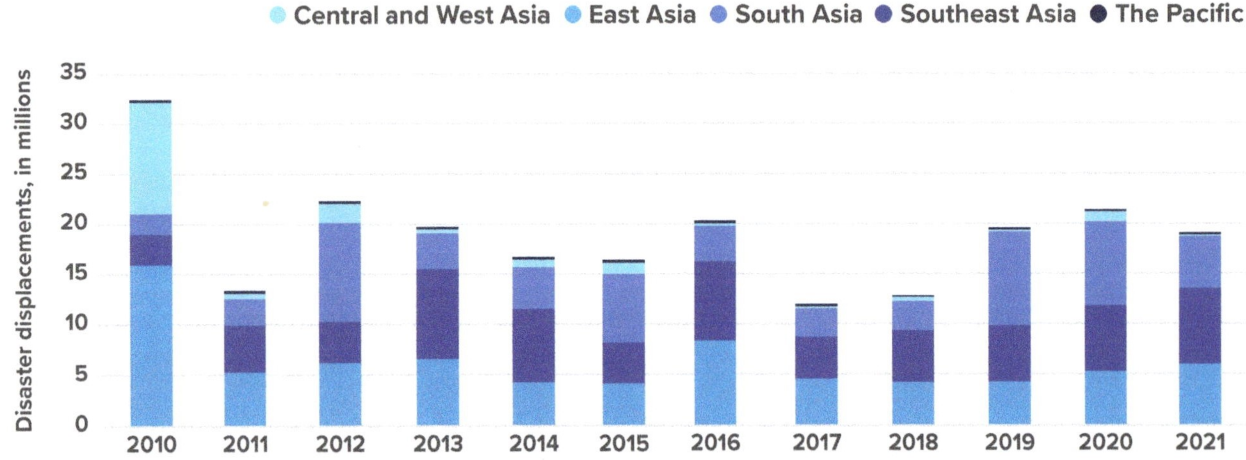

Figure 2: Internal Displacements by Disasters per Subregion (2010–2021)

Source: Internal Displacement Monitoring Centre, 2022

Breakdown of Disaster Displacement by Hazard

Weather-related hazards, such as monsoon rains, floods, storms, and cyclones, were responsible for 95% of all disaster displacements across the region between 2010–2021 (Figure 3). Although less frequent, geophysical events such as earthquakes, tsunamis, and volcanic eruptions triggered an estimated 11.8 million internal displacements, equivalent to 5.2% of the total. Displacement associated with slow-onset hazards including riverbank erosion, extreme temperatures, droughts, and glacial melt has also been reported across the region, with 760,000 internal displacements, or 0.3% of the total. However, this is a significant underestimate, given the lack of data on slow-onset hazards.

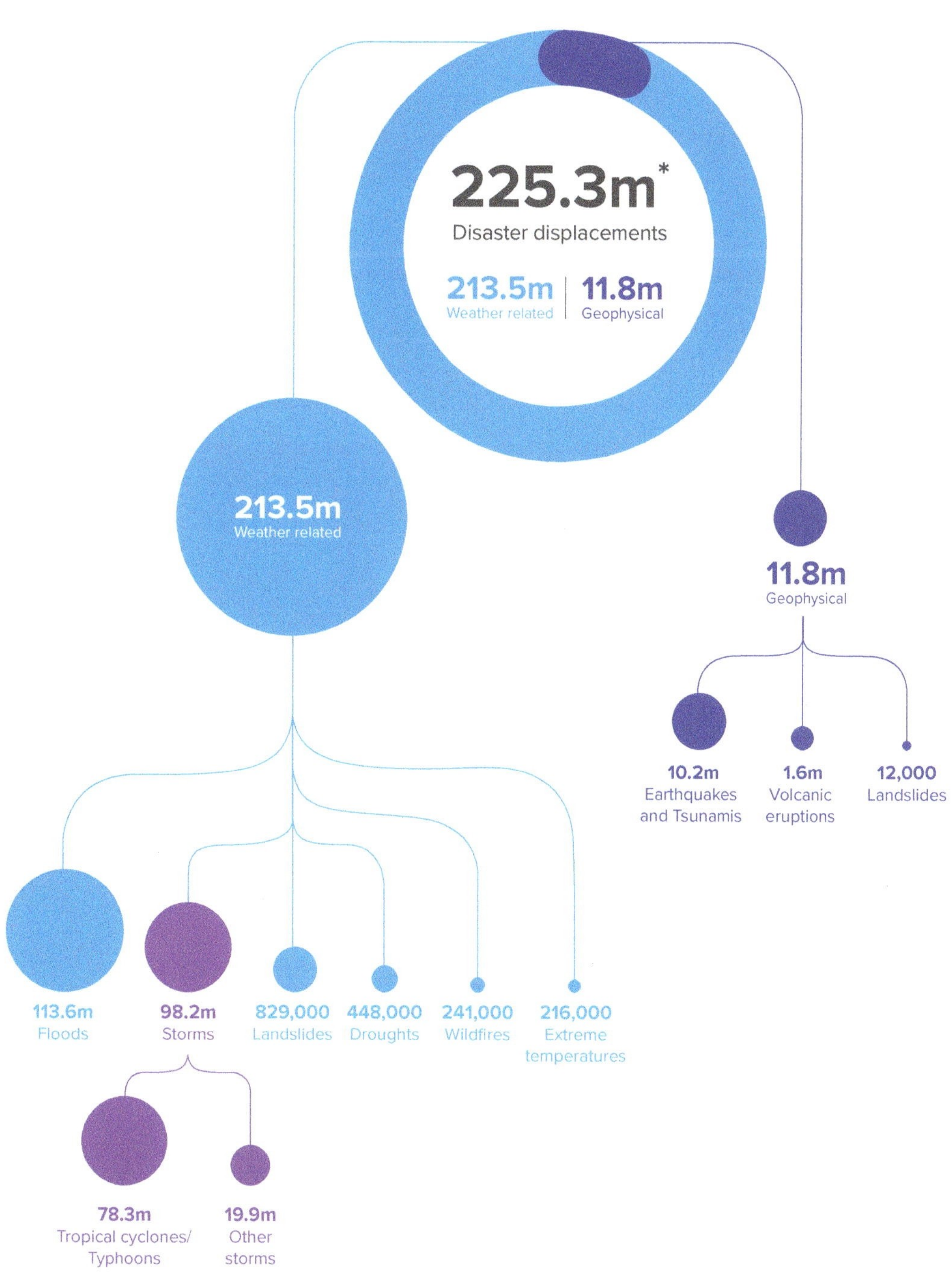

Figure 3: Internal Displacements in Asia and the Pacific: Breakdown by Hazard (2010–2021)

Source: Internal Displacement Monitoring Centre, 2022

Floods

Figure 4: Three Largest Displacement Events Caused by Floods

1 | **Floods, 2010**
People's Republic of China
15.5m

2 | **Floods, 2010**
Pakistan
11m

3 | **Floods, 2012**
India
8.9m

Three Countries with Most Internal Displacements Caused by Floods

1 | **People's Republic of China**
40.4m

2 | **India**
29.9m

3 | **Pakistan**
15.2m

The rainfall brought on by monsoon seasons has played an important role in the social and economic development of the region by supporting agriculture development, generating energy, and sustaining the livelihoods of millions of people. However, excessive rainfall—combined with human factors—has also caused devastating riverine as well as coastal and flash floods, uprooting millions of people every year across the region. Floods have been the hazard triggering most disaster displacements in Asia and the Pacific since 2010, with 113.6 million, or 50% of the total.

Most displacements associated with floods are urban, as cities are often located in flood-prone river basins or coastal areas.[4] Rapid urbanization in highly populated countries like Bangladesh, India, and the PRC has contributed to heightened flood displacement risk, especially in unplanned and informal settlements that lack adequate drainage and water management infrastructure. As a result, poor communities tend to be unevenly affected by the impacts of floods and resulting displacement.[5]

Other human-driven factors such as the widespread destruction of coastal mangroves in the Pacific or the construction of large dams in Southeast Asia, have rendered countries more prone to floods.[6] This has been the case, for instance, in countries located along the Mekong River—Cambodia, the Lao People's Democratic Republic, Myanmar,[7] the PRC, Thailand, and Viet Nam—where dam failures and releases have played a role in driving flood displacement risk.[8]

Flood displacement is expected to continue as urbanization and infrastructure development increase. According to the IDMC global disaster displacement risk model, 17.8 million people worldwide are at risk of being displaced by floods every year, 80% of whom live in urban and peri-urban areas. Such risk is mostly concentrated in South Asia, East Asia, and the Pacific.[9] Although not included in the model, global warming and population growth are projected to increase flood displacement risk significantly.[10]

Homes underwater in India. Villagers paddle their boat near submerged houses close to the Kaziranga National Park, Assam. Floods in northeastern India forced millions of people to flee their homes in 2012. (Photo by Biju Boro/AFP/Getty Images)

Figure 5: Three Largest Displacement Events Caused by Storms

1 | **Typhoon Haiyan, 2013**
Palau, People's Republic of China, Philippines, Viet Nam
5.1m

2 | **Cyclone Amphan, 2020**
Bangladesh, Bhutan, India, Myanmar
5m

3 | **Typhoon Rai, 2021**
Palau, Philippines, Viet Nam
3.9m

Three Countries with Most Internal Displacements Caused by Storms

1 | **Philippines**
41m

2 | **People's Republic of China**
27.1m

3 | **India**
11.3m

Storms triggered 98.2 million internal displacements in the region during 2010–2021. Tropical cyclones—also referred to in the region as typhoons—account for 80% of total storm-related displacement. They bring high levels of rainfall causing floods, destructive wind gusts, and storm surges that destroy housing and infrastructure and disrupt basic service provision.

Although many of the displacements triggered by high-intensity storms are government-led pre-emptive evacuations to avoid loss of life and injury, all too often their devastating impacts leave entire areas uninhabitable, prolonging the displacement of those who moved. Post-disaster needs assessments provide information on the economic costs of these major disasters, but the wider economic impacts of displacement—including its protracted nature—tend to go unaccounted for. This leaves a significant information gap on the direct, indirect, and long-term impacts of displacement.

Figure 6 shows the areas in which tropical cyclones formed during 2010–2021, and some of the cyclones that triggered displacement. Hotspots are located in areas between the tropics, exposing populations in East and Southeast Asia, the Arabian Sea and the Bay of Bengal in South Asia, and the Pacific.

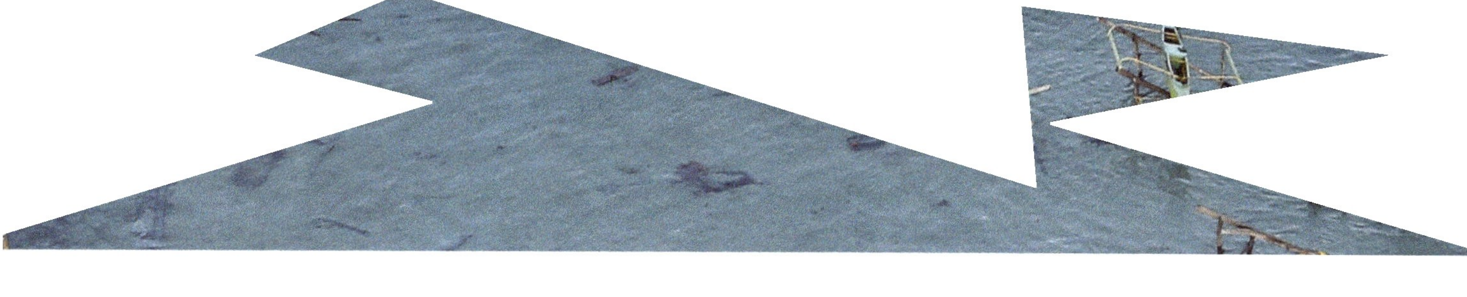

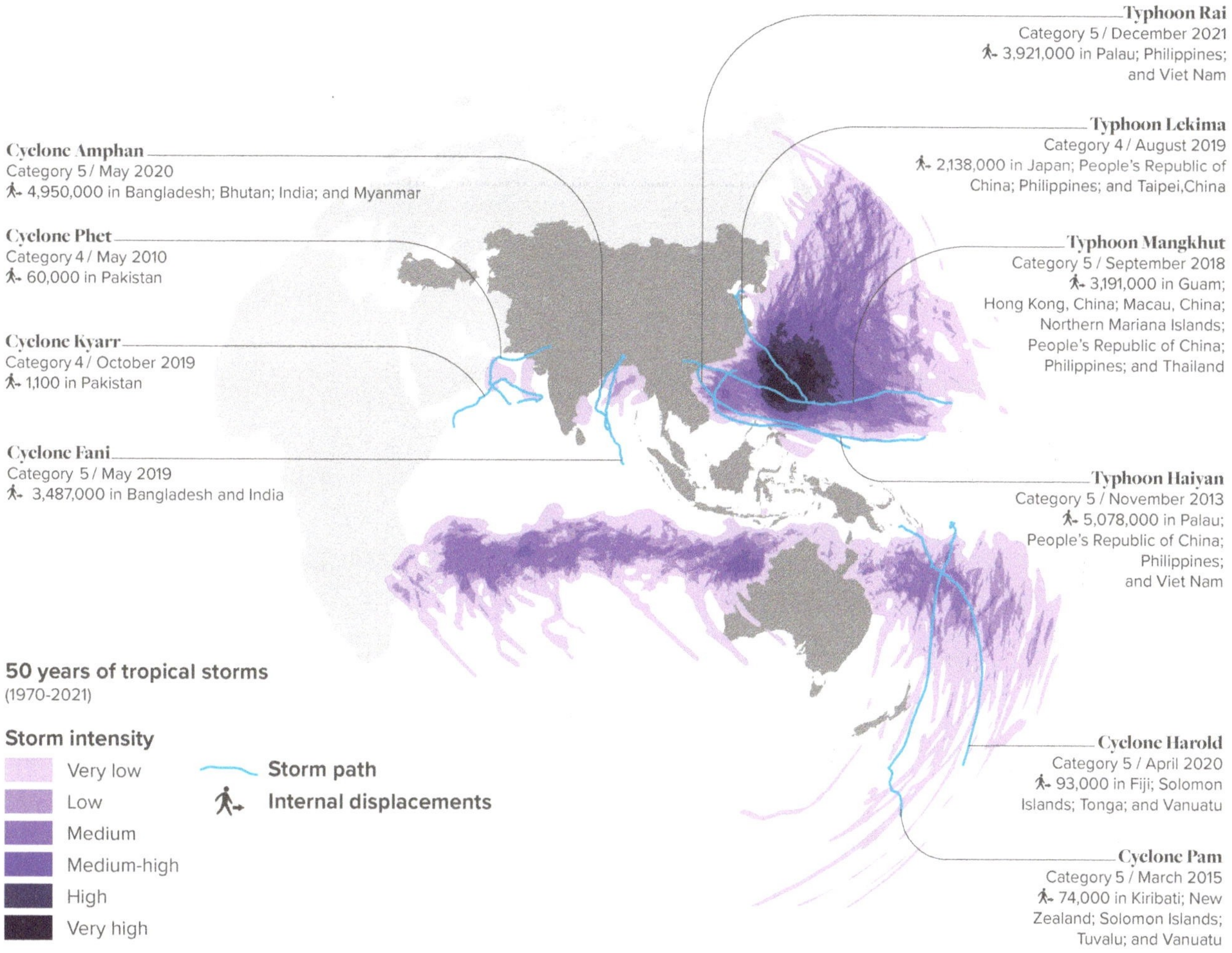

Typhoon Rai
Category 5 / December 2021
3,921,000 in Palau; Philippines; and Viet Nam

Typhoon Lekima
Category 4 / August 2019
2,138,000 in Japan; People's Republic of China; Philippines; and Taipei,China

Typhoon Mangkhut
Category 5 / September 2018
3,191,000 in Guam; Hong Kong, China; Macau, China; Northern Mariana Islands; People's Republic of China; Philippines; and Thailand

Cyclone Amphan
Category 5 / May 2020
4,950,000 in Bangladesh; Bhutan; India; and Myanmar

Cyclone Phet
Category 4 / May 2010
60,000 in Pakistan

Cyclone Kyarr
Category 4 / October 2019
1,100 in Pakistan

Cyclone Fani
Category 5 / May 2019
3,487,000 in Bangladesh and India

Typhoon Haiyan
Category 5 / November 2013
5,078,000 in Palau; People's Republic of China; Philippines; and Viet Nam

50 years of tropical storms
(1970-2021)

Storm intensity
Very low
Low
Medium
Medium-high
High
Very high

Storm path
Internal displacements

Cyclone Harold
Category 5 / April 2020
93,000 in Fiji; Solomon Islands; Tonga; and Vanuatu

Cyclone Pam
Category 5 / March 2015
74,000 in Kiribati; New Zealand; Solomon Islands; Tuvalu; and Vanuatu

Figure 6: Frequency of Tropical Cyclones and Events Triggering Displacement in the Asia and Pacific Region (2010–2021)

Source: Internal Displacement Monitoring Centre, 2022; Preview Global Risk Data Platform; NOAA International Best Track Archive for Climate Stewardship (IBTrACS)

Coastal town demolished by Typhoon Haiyan. A town on Eastern Samar Island in Leyte, Philippines, after Typhoon Haiyan hit the area in November 2013. The typhoon has been described as one of the most powerful ones ever to hit land, leaving hundreds of thousands without a home (Photo by Dan Kitwood/Getty Images)

Figure 7: Three Largest Displacement Events Caused by Earthquakes and Tsunamis

1 | **Gorkha Earthquake, 2015**
Nepal
2.6m

2 | **Hindu Kush Earthquake, 2015**
Afghanistan
720,000

3 | **Lushan Earthquake, 2013**
People's Republic of China
695,000

Three Countries with Most Internal Displacements Caused by Earthquakes and Tsunamis

1 | **Nepal**
2.7m

2 | **People's Republic of China**
2.6m

3 | **Indonesia**
1.4m

Asia and the Pacific is the world's most active seismic region.[11] Several countries are located along the Pacific Ring of Fire—where tectonic plates meet—triggering around 90% of the earthquakes globally. Indonesia, Japan, Papua New Guinea, and the Philippines are particularly at risk of seismic activity, including tsunamis.[12] Other countries in continental Asia are highly prone to earthquakes due to the collision of the Indian and Eurasian plates.

Although less frequent than tropical cyclones or floods, the impacts of earthquakes and tsunamis can be devastating. Combined, they triggered 10.2 million internal displacements during 2010–2021. High population growth, rapid urbanization, and inadequate planning in the region's earthquake-prone areas heightened displacement impacts in countries like Indonesia, Pakistan, and the PRC.[13]

Earthquakes can also cause other hazards including tsunamis, avalanches, landslides, and liquefaction, the combined effects of which can trigger or prolong displacement. In Nepal, for example, the 2015 Gorkha earthquake and the following aftershocks triggered landslides and avalanches, displacing 2.6 million people. In 2018, a 7.5 magnitude earthquake hit the Central Sulawesi province of Indonesia that triggered liquefaction, mudflows, and a tsunami, showing how geophysical hazards can have cascading impacts.[14]

[a] ADB placed on hold its assistance in Afghanistan effective 15 August 2021. ADB Statement on Afghanistan (published on 10 November 2021). No consultations or engagements took place after 31 July 2021.

Earthquakes were the second-most costly disaster in the Asia and Pacific region during 2010–2021.[15] However, as for other disasters, the economic impacts of internal displacement remain largely unknown, as reporting on damages and losses often stops shortly after they strike, hampering understanding of how livelihoods and productivity loss represent a burden to people and the broader economy.

Devastation caused by an earthquake. Damaged trees lie at the foot of a landslide triggered by a powerful 6.7 magnitude earthquake in Atsuma on the northern Japanese island of Hokkaido. (Photo by Carl Court/Getty Images)

Figure 8: Three Largest Displacement Events Caused by Volcanic Eruptions

1 | **Mount Taal Eruption, 2020**
Philippines
506,000

2 | **Mount Merapi Eruption, 2010**
Indonesia
361,000

3 | **Mount Agung Eruption, 2017**
Indonesia
150,000

Three Countries with Most Internal Displacements Caused by Volcanic Eruptions

1 | **Indonesia**
869,000

2 | **Philippines**
672,000

3 | **Papua New Guinea**
28,000

The Asia and Pacific region—and more particularly the Pacific Ring of Fire—has 75% of all active volcanoes in the world. Beyond lava flows, volcanic eruptions can cause ash clouds, pyroclastic flows (lava fragments and gases ejected explosively from a volcano), and lahars (volcanic mudflows) that can have devastating effects.[16] Since 2010, there have been 1.6 million internal displacements triggered by volcanic activity across 6 countries (Indonesia, Japan, New Zealand, Papua New Guinea, the Philippines, and Vanuatu).

Local and national authorities across the region are taking steps to limit the potential human toll of volcanic eruptions. In the Philippines, the government pre-emptively evacuated 506,000 people days and hours before the Taal volcano erupted in early 2020. Displacements in the form of evacuations were also an important life-saving measure in September 2017, when the Meteorology and Geo-Hazards Department of Vanuatu announced the possible eruption of Manaro Voui on the island of Ambae. Faced with an event that potentially put the whole island at risk, the government took extraordinary steps to protect its population by evacuating 11,000 people from high-risk areas.[17]

Depending on its intensity and damages and losses caused, volcanic activity can prolong the displacement of people, as their homes, land, and crops can be destroyed and their livelihoods disrupted.

Volcanic eruption. Dead trees covered in volcanic ash from the Taal Volcano eruption in the Philippines in 2020. Authorities evacuated tens of thousands of people from the area. (Photo by Ezra Acayan/Getty Images)

Figure 9: Three Largest Displacement Events Caused by Slow-Onset Hazards

1 | **Drought, 2018**
Afghanistan
371,000

2 | **Extreme Temperatures, 2011**
People's Republic of China
88,000

3 | **Winter Storm, 2016**
People's Republic of China
78,000

Three Countries with Most Internal Displacements Caused by Slow-Onset Hazards

1 | **Afghanistan**
389,000

2 | **People's Republic of China**
184,000

3 | **India**
68,000

Melting glaciers, coastal erosion, droughts, slow-onset hazards, and the effects of climate change are a reality across the region.[18] It is difficult to paint a consistent picture of displacement associated with slow-onset events, because of the wide range of phenomena, impacts, drivers, types of movement they cause, and countries they affect.[19] During 2010–2021, at least 760,000 internal displacements were identified in 17 countries and territories across the Asia and Pacific region.

Below-average monsoon rains can cause severe droughts which affect rural communities whose livelihoods depend on agriculture. This is especially true where rainfall is the only source of water for agricultural production. During 2018–2021, droughts caused 448,000 internal displacements in Afghanistan, India, Mongolia, Pakistan, and the Philippines.[20]

The most significant event took place in Afghanistan in 2018, when more than 371,000 internal displacements due to drought were reported. After 4 years of below-average rainfall in the north-western provinces, large numbers of people began to move from rural to urban areas in search of livelihood opportunities, basic services, and humanitarian aid.[21] A similar reality was observed again in 2021 when a nationwide drought was declared in June.[22] Food insecurity and water scarcity increased, heightening the needs of those affected, including internally displaced persons (IDPs).[23]

The impact of slow-onset disasters is particularly important for small island developing states in the Pacific, where sea-level rise, coastal erosion, and salinization pose an existential threat to communities living in low-lying atolls. These hazards are often compounded by sudden-onset hazards such as cyclones and storm surges, which can further undermine livelihoods and force people to flee either temporarily or relocate permanently to higher ground or larger islands.[24]

Coastal and riverbank erosion is another type of slow-onset hazard that compounds with sudden-onset events like floods and other human-driven factors including damming, deforestation, and land degradation. During 2010–2021, erosion caused about 89,000 internal displacements across the region, most of them in Bangladesh, Pakistan, and the Philippines.

As slow-onset events unfold across the Asia and Pacific region, however, their impacts and outcomes are not only shaped by the hazards themselves. They are largely determined by the vulnerability of people and the effectiveness of investments in disaster risk reduction, climate change adaptation, and sustainable development. The economic resilience of individuals and communities will play a role in the likelihood of displacement from happening in such contexts, and for some, moving may not even be an option. Perceptions of risk, individual and cultural preferences, attachment to a community and place, aspirations, and expectations of areas of destination will all play a role.[25]

Forced to move on. NRC distributes tents to families uprooted by drought in Badghis, Afghanistan in 2018. (Photo by Enayatullah Azad/NRC)

Subregional Overviews

On flooded roads in Pakistan. In August 2010, floods forced hundreds of thousands of people to leave their homes in one of the worst disasters in Pakistan's history. (Photo by Daniel Berehulak via Getty Images)

33.7% of the regional total

The high population density of East Asia is a major driver of disaster displacement risk. The region is home to an estimated 1.6 billion people accounting for more than 20% of the entire global population.[26] East Asia has been experiencing increasing urbanization, especially in the People's Republic of China (PRC), where the percentage of people living in cities has gone from 49% in 2010 to 61% in 2020.[27]

In addition to a high population exposure through increasing urbanization, East Asia is prone to a range of hazards including storms, floods, earthquakes, and tsunamis, which also contribute to making it a disaster displacement risk hotspot. Over one-third of the 225.3 million disaster displacements recorded in the Asia and Pacific region between 2010 and 2021 took place in East Asia, with the PRC alone accounting for 70.4 million (Figure 11).

Floods caused over half of the disaster displacements in East Asia. The 2010 floods in the PRC were the worst over the period, triggering 15.5 million displacements across three-quarters of the country's provinces.[28] Multiple intense hazards prompted the government to move from a reactive to a proactive approach to disaster risk management.[29]

The government also introduced a "sponge city" initiative in 2014 to minimize the risk of urban flooding. The idea is to reduce hard-surface areas in cities and increase permeable areas—such as rain gardens, green roofs, and constructed wetlands—which mitigate surface-water flooding and peak run-off and improve the purification of urban runoff and water conservation.[30] In some cities like Zhengzhou, the introduction of sponge city infrastructure has reduced flooding in 125 areas and recycled 380 million tons of water.[31] As a result, since 2017 the city has been recording fewer displacements during the May to September rainy season.[32]

Displacement continues to be a challenge, especially in the context of severe disasters that hit highly urbanized areas. In July 2021, Zhengzhou experienced the worst floods in 1,000 years when the equivalent of a year's rainfall fell in 3 days, overwhelming the city's capacity to absorb water and forcing 1.5 million people from their homes. This single event triggered one-quarter of the total internal displacements recorded in the PRC that year. The Zhengzhou sponge city infrastructure likely helped reduce the scale and duration of floods, despite its limitations.[33] Comprehensive standards, national guidelines, and increased financial and human resources will be needed to make cities in the PRC more resilient to future climate shocks.[34] Given that almost all major cities are exposed to frequent flooding, this should be a priority as extreme weather events become more frequent and intense.[35]

Many flood-related displacements have been the result of major storms, which tend to take place between July and September. During 2010–2021, storms led to about 30.4 million disaster displacements (Figure 12). Typhoon Lekima—which made landfall in the Zhejiang Province of the PRC in August 2019—triggered the highest number of internal displacements in East Asia that year. It was also the deadliest and costliest storm in the whole Asia and Pacific region that year, with economic losses estimated at USD 10 billion.[36]

East Asia is also prone to seismic activity.[37] The Great East Japan earthquake and tsunami that hit the Fukushima prefecture in March 2011 is a case in point. This event was significant not only because of the deaths and high damage to housing and infrastructure, but because it left most internally displaced people in conditions of protracted displacement. The disaster triggered as many as 492,000 displacements. A study carried out by IDMC in 2017 estimated that as many as 134,000 people were still displaced 6 years following the event.[38] As of the end of 2021, 39,000 people remained displaced.[39]

East Asia has also experienced periods of extended droughts and harsh winters. For instance, Mongolia has been increasingly affected by the impacts of the dzud,[40] where temperatures can drop to as low as −50°C across the country, which leads to mass livestock loss and disrupts the livelihoods of thousands of nomadic communities.[41] Climate change and the overgrazing of the Mongolian steppe have largely contributed to increasing the impacts of the dzud.[42] These severe winter conditions

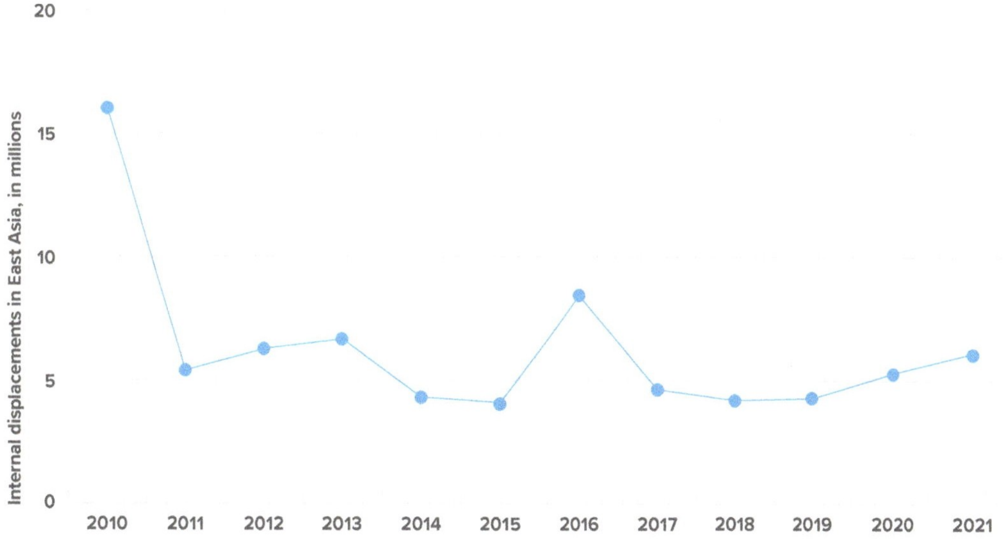

Figure 10: Internal Displacements by Disasters in East Asia (2010–2021)

Source: Internal Displacement Monitoring Centre, 2022

caused approximately 1,000 displacements, a figure that should be considered an underestimate.

Climate change and environmental degradation will continue to have significant impacts on the millions of people who live on deltas, coastlines, and other low-lying areas prone to riverine and coastal flooding, salinization, and erosion.[43] Other slow-onset hazards, including desertification and glacier melt, may also function as drivers of rural-to-urban displacement, thereby increasing urbanization. Cities will therefore continue to play a central role in building future sustainable development and reducing disaster displacement risk.

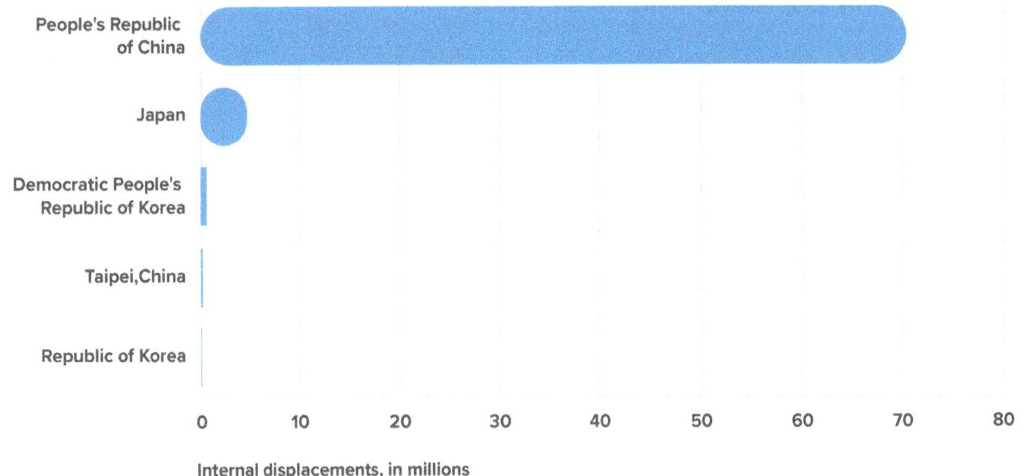

Figure 11: Five Economies with the most Disaster Displacements in East Asia (2010–2021)

Source: Internal Displacement Monitoring Centre, 2022

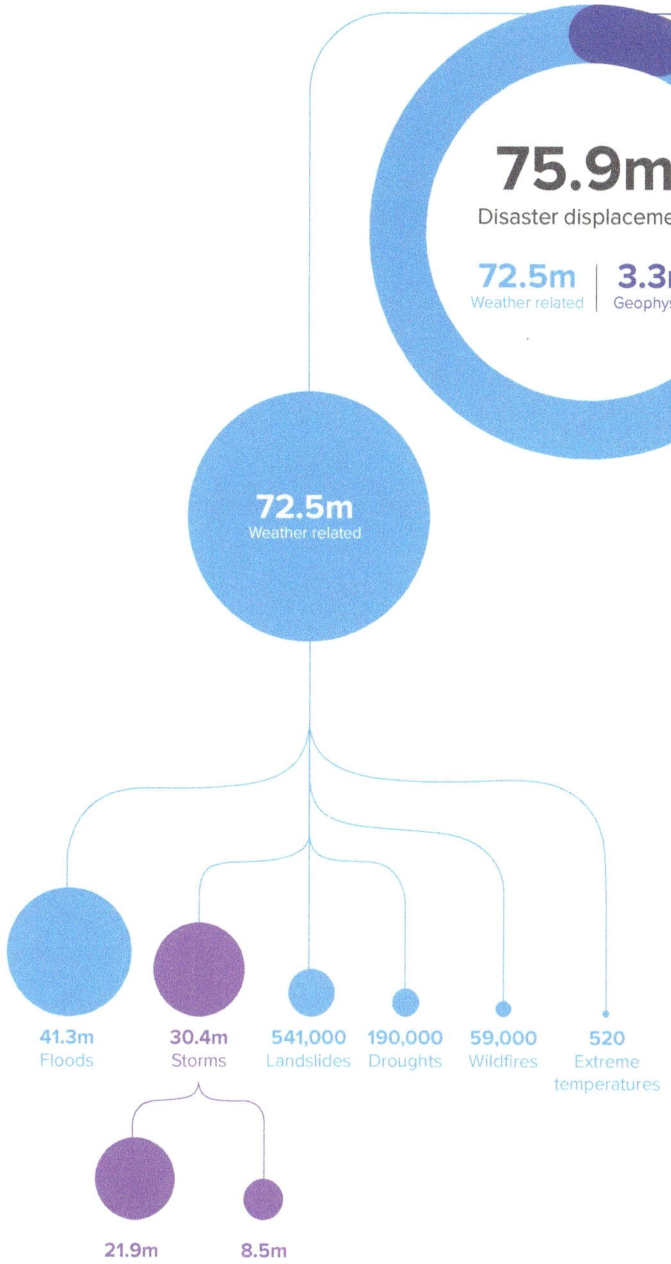

75.9m*
Disaster displacements

72.5m Weather related | 3.3m Geophysical

72.5m
Weather related

41.3m Floods
30.4m Storms
21.9m
8.5m
541,000 Landslides
190,000 Droughts
59,000 Wildfires
520 Extreme temperatures

3.3m
Geophysical

3.3m Earthquakes and Tsunamis
1,900 Volcanic eruptions
360 Landslides

Figure 12: Disaster Displacements in East Asia: Breakdown by Hazard (2010–2021)

Source: Internal Displacement Monitoring Centre, 2022

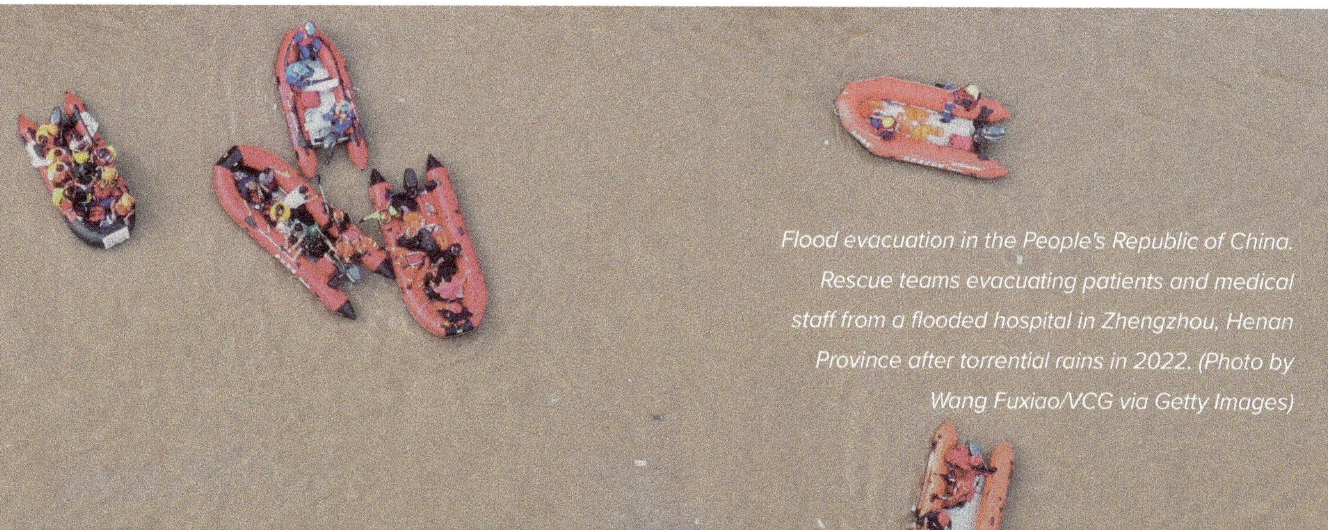

Flood evacuation in the People's Republic of China. Rescue teams evacuating patients and medical staff from a flooded hospital in Zhengzhou, Henan Province after torrential rains in 2022. (Photo by Wang Fuxiao/VCG via Getty Images)

30.7% of the regional total

Countries across Southeast Asia also rank as some of the most hazard-prone in the Asia and Pacific region and globally, as many are located along the Pacific Ring of Fire and the region's Typhoon Belt, exposing its inhabitants to a wide variety of hazards including seasonal storms and floods, volcanic eruptions, earthquakes, and tsunamis. Southeast Asia's population growth is mirrored by economic growth which has concentrated people and economic activities in urban areas, often located in hazard-prone areas.

Almost 31% of the total disaster displacement recorded in the Asia and Pacific region during 2020–2021 has been reported in Southeast Asia. The Philippines has been the country most affected, as it experiences between 5 and 10 destructive tropical cyclones every year, making it one of the countries most at risk of extreme weather events in the Asia and Pacific region and globally.[44]

During 2010–2021, nearly 49.3 million displacements were reported in the Philippines, mostly triggered by storms (Figure 14). One of the most severe was typhoon Haiyan in 2013. Haiyan ravaged large areas of the country, triggering 4.1 million displacements, more than one-fifth of the 19.7 million disaster displacements reported in the Asia and Pacific region that year.[45] Its scale and impacts paved the way for stronger disaster risk reduction mechanisms, including the improvement of early warning systems and evacuation protocols.[46]

Efforts paid off when typhoon Rai—also known as Odette—struck the country in 2021. Authorities pre-emptively evacuated most of the 3.9 million people displaced over 1 week ahead of its landfall.[47] Although disaster mortality was reduced, the damages brought on by Rai were of a comparable scale to those reported during Haiyan. The storm destroyed around 415,000 homes across the archipelago and damaged around 1.7 million of them. IDP livelihoods were also disrupted and food prices increased, heightening the risk of food insecurity.[48] More than 590,000 people were still displaced by Rai as of the end of 2021. This shows that despite progress in preparedness activities to reduce population exposure and vulnerability, recovering from disasters—including limiting the duration of displacement of the people pre-emptively evacuated—continues to be a significant challenge.

Viet Nam faces a similar reality, as all of the 3,260 km coastline is at high risk of cyclones and storm surges.[49] Consecutive or overlapping storms and floods often hit the country, putting hundreds of thousands into displacement every year. For example, in October and November 2020, the tropical cyclone season overlapped with the monsoon season, and seven consecutive tropical storms and cyclones hit the country, leading to historical floods. As a result, Viet Nam recorded close to 1.3 million internal displacements in 2020, the highest number for the country ever recorded.

Many communities and countries are also grappling with low human development, and social and economic vulnerability play a role in heightening disaster displacement risk.[50] In Timor-Leste, for example, 42% of the population lives below the poverty line, and poor people tend to live in hazard-prone areas at a higher risk of disaster displacement.[51] When tropical storm Seroja struck the country in April 2021, close to 16,000 people were forced to seek shelter, and many lost their homes and were still displaced as the year concluded.[52]

The expansion of cities has further increased flood displacement risk across Southeast Asia, particularly in areas ill-planned to withstand the impact of hazards. This is the case in the Jakarta Metropolitan Area in Indonesia, where every year, thousands of people are evacuated from their homes because of flooding caused by torrential rains. The city—which sits on a swamp—is home to more than 30 million people and is the second-largest megacity in the world. Sea-level rise, construction on land prone to subsidence, and reliance on pumping groundwater are contributing to the sinking of Jakarta.[53] Plans to move the city to a safer location in East Kalimantan are underway as of 2022.[54]

Although weather-related hazards have triggered most of the displacement, Southeast Asian countries are also prone to earthquakes and volcanic eruptions that could trigger mass displacement in the years and decades to come. 97% of the total 1.6 million disaster displacements

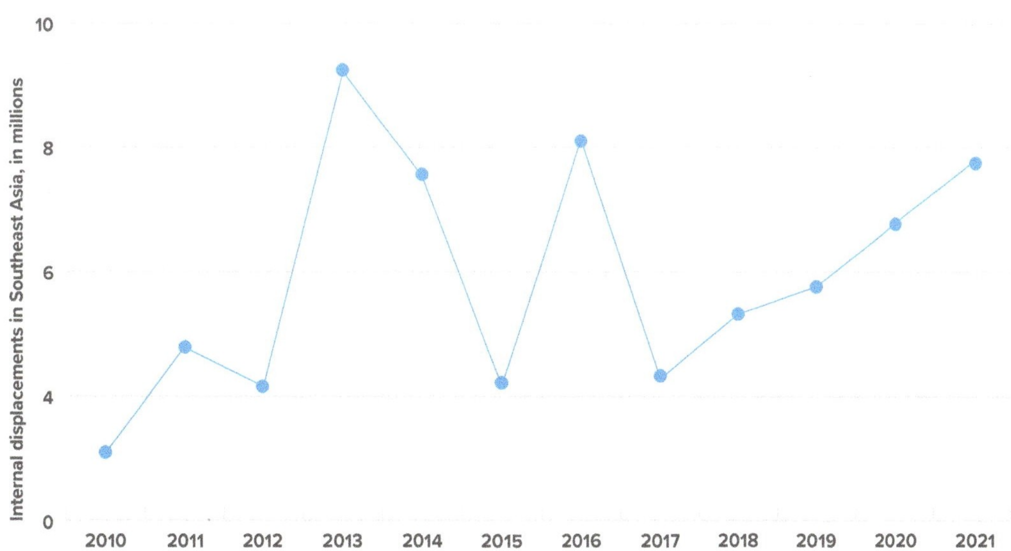

Figure 13: Internal Displacements by Disasters in Southeast Asia (2010–2021)

Source: Internal Displacement Monitoring Centre, 2022

triggered by volcanic eruptions during 2010–2021 in Asia and the Pacific were recorded in the Philippines and Indonesia, both of which have sound monitoring systems to track volcanic activity and move people out of harm's way (Figure 15).

Countries in Southeast Asia are particularly affected by disasters, a trend that is also expected to continue well into the future. The impacts of climate change such as sea-level rise—which is projected to inundate 40% of the Mekong Delta—and drought will hamper the livelihoods of millions of people.[55] These hazards, coupled with increasing urbanization and the damming of major rivers, can compound and trigger further displacement. For countries affected by conflict and violence—including Myanmar and the Philippines—conflict and disaster displacement can also overlap, aggravating the impacts on those displaced.[56] Longer-term, sustainable urbanization and development will be key to reducing displacement overall risk.

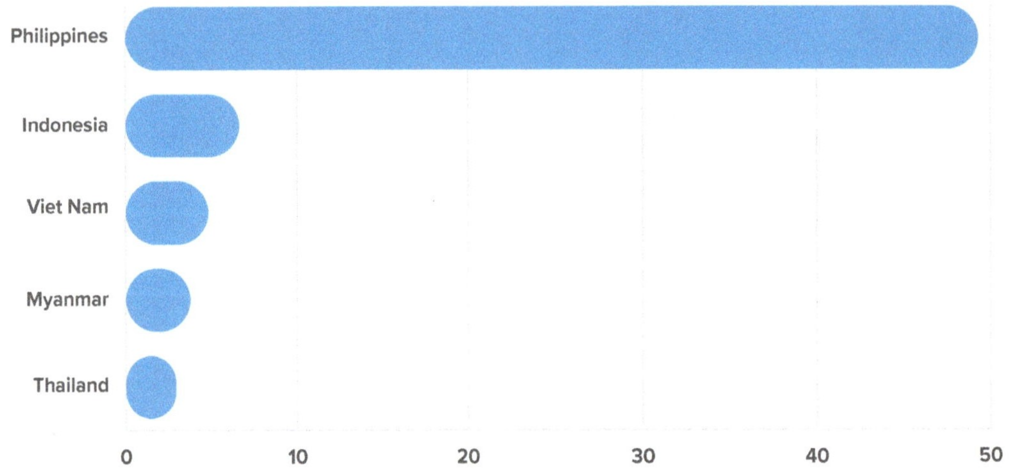

Figure 14: Five Countries and Territories with the most Disaster Displacements in Southeast Asia (2010–2021)

Source: Internal Displacement Monitoring Centre, 2022

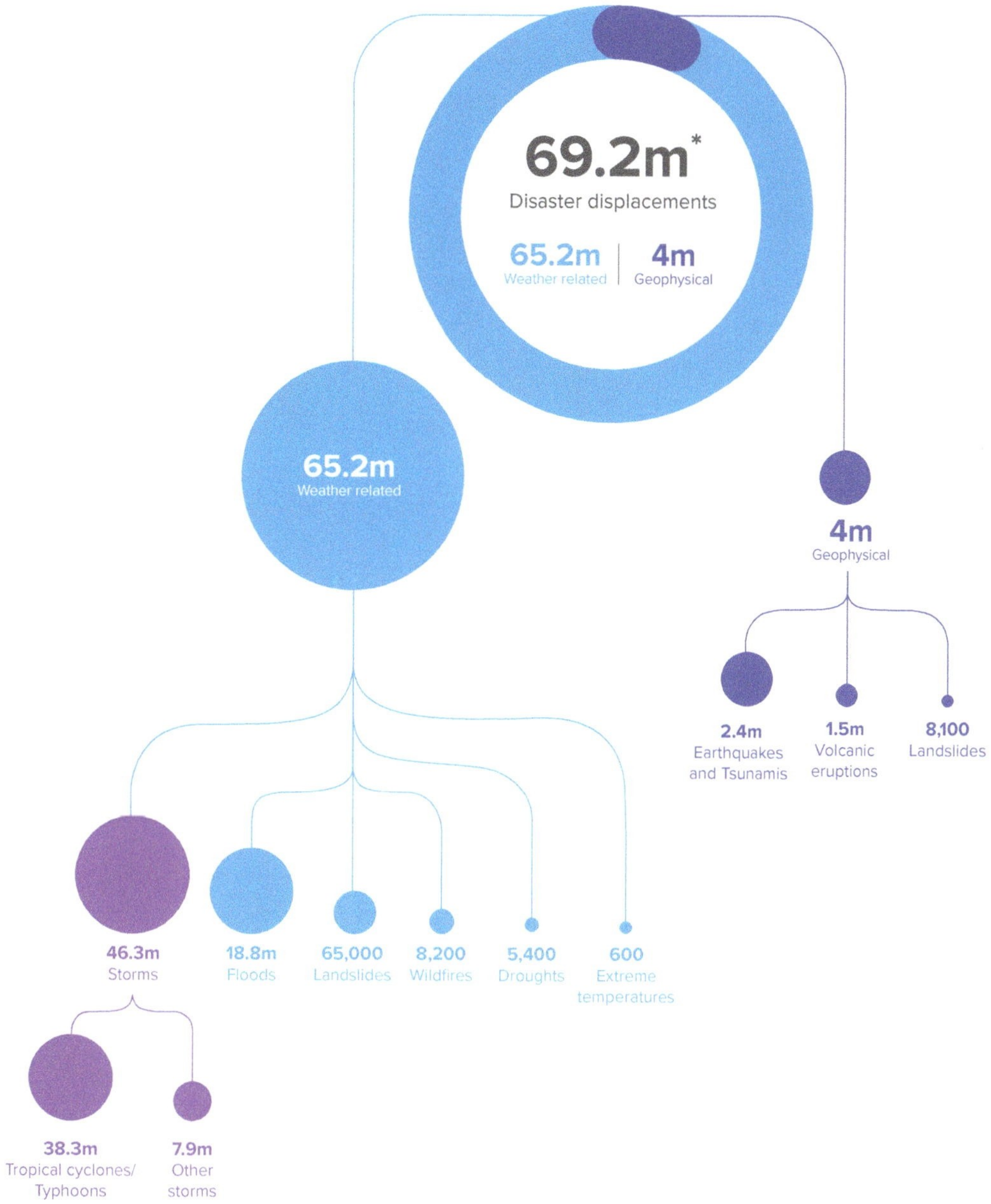

69.2m*
Disaster displacements

65.2m
Weather related

4m
Geophysical

65.2m
Weather related

4m
Geophysical

46.3m
Storms

18.8m
Floods

65,000
Landslides

8,200
Wildfires

5,400
Droughts

600
Extreme temperatures

38.3m
Tropical cyclones/ Typhoons

7.9m
Other storms

2.4m
Earthquakes and Tsunamis

1.5m
Volcanic eruptions

8,100
Landslides

Figure 15: Disaster Displacements in Southeast Asia: Breakdown by Hazard (2010–2021)

Source: Internal Displacement Monitoring Centre, 2022

South Asia

27.3% of the regional total

Despite experiencing rapid economic growth and some of the highest annual urbanization rates in the world, South Asian countries are still grappling with low social and economic development, leaving millions of people with a limited capacity to cope with the effects of disasters and climate change.[57] Socioeconomic vulnerability—coupled with population growth in areas prone to hazards—drives disaster displacement risk across the subregion, including in some of its megacities such as Mumbai and Dhaka.[58]

South Asia accounted for the third-largest share of disaster displacement during 2010–2021 in the Asia and Pacific region, with 61.4 million disaster displacements. From India to Bangladesh, and from Nepal to Sri Lanka, floods, storms, and earthquakes drive mass displacement every year (Figure 17). Millions of these displacements are in the form of pre-emptive evacuations, a testament to increased efforts in disaster preparedness by governments. Nonetheless, in coastal areas and low-lying riverbanks, recurring and destructive storms force people to repeatedly flee, sometimes for prolonged periods.

A third of the displacements associated with floods in the Asia and Pacific region take place in South Asia, mostly during the annual Southwest and Northeast monsoon seasons.[59] In recent years, the region has experienced shifts in flood duration, and the El Niño Southern Oscillation variation has also played a role in their frequency and intensity.[60]

In 2021, La Niña weakened the South Asia monsoon season, which in turn forced fewer people from their homes than in previous years.[61] However, in India the Southwest monsoon season lasted from June to October—instead of September—overlapping with the onset of the Northeast monsoon.[62] This rare phenomenon brought unusually heavy rains and floods to several southern Indian states and triggered 312,000 displacements in Tamil Nadu in November. As climate change contributes to more prolonged and erratic monsoon seasons, the impact of seasonal flooding in South Asia may continue to have devastating consequences.[63]

Storms—including major tropical cyclones—triggered about 21 million internal displacements during 2010–2021 (Figure 18). Seasonal changes in wind direction and warmer temperatures in the Indian Ocean fuel these powerful cyclones, most of which happen on the edge of the monsoon season. The most significant storm to affect the region in recent years was Cyclone Amphan, which formed in the Bay of Bengal in May 2020 and triggered close to 5 million displacements in India and Bangladesh. Thousands remained displaced in Bangladesh 1 year later, many of whom may have been pushed into secondary displacement as cyclone Yaas hit in May 2021.[64] In addition, rising sea levels are causing more devastating storm surges, which impact an increasing number of people living along coastal areas.[65]

Structural measures to mitigate the impacts of storms—such as embankments—have contributed to increasing displacement risk in several locations across South Asia.[66] The false

Programme and Central Emergency Response Fund are using forecasts to help people prepare for the next climate shock in Bangladesh. (Photo by WFP/ Sayed Asif Mahmud)

sense of protection created by these traditional infrastructural measures allowed for even more unregulated activities in flood-prone areas, including the construction of informal settlements. This, in turn, has contributed to increasing the exposure of people to floods.[67] In 2017, severe flooding left thousands displaced in Dhaka, one of the fastest-growing cities in South Asia. The city has expanded over marshlands leaving no space for water run-off and exacerbating the impact of flooding.[68] Embankment failures and collapses caused by large storm surges have also exacerbated displacement due to flooding in areas already hit by recurring disasters.[69]

As much of the subregion sits on the collision point between three tectonic plates, South Asia is one of the most seismically active regions in the world. Urban growth and the lack of building regulations have rendered urban populations more vulnerable to earthquakes than in the past.[70] As a result, earthquakes triggered 2.9 million internal displacements during 2010–2021, 92% of which took place due to the Gorkha earthquake in Nepal. The seismic movement caused by this single earthquake changed the geological layout of the landscape in mountainous areas, which increased the risk of landslides in several villages. These cascading impacts materialized in the form of disasters, and communities have been displaced as a result. Further displacement risk is expected in the event of a future major earthquake.[71]

The combination of seismic and climate risks keeps representing a challenge for South Asian countries. Impacts like floods, storms, and glacial lake outburst floods can

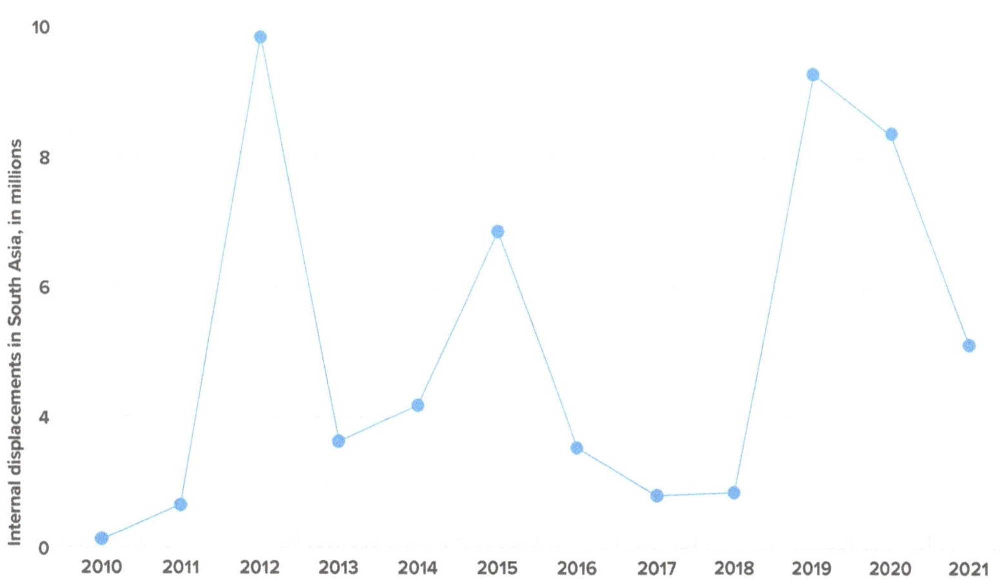

Figure 16: Internal Displacements by Disasters in South Asia (2010–2021)

Source: Internal Displacement Monitoring Centre, 2022

have transboundary impacts and trigger further displacement.[72] Knowing that this represents a potential barrier to sustainable development, governments have made significant efforts in strengthening disaster risk at local and regional levels. Opportunities like the Bay of Bengal Initiative for Multi-Sectoral and Economic Cooperation, and the Coalition for Disaster Resilient Infrastructure, provide an entry point for governments to mitigate the impact of disasters in South Asia.[73] Promoting a whole-of-society approach—by facilitating participation among marginalized and vulnerable populations—will also be key, as they often face the highest exposure to disasters and displacement.

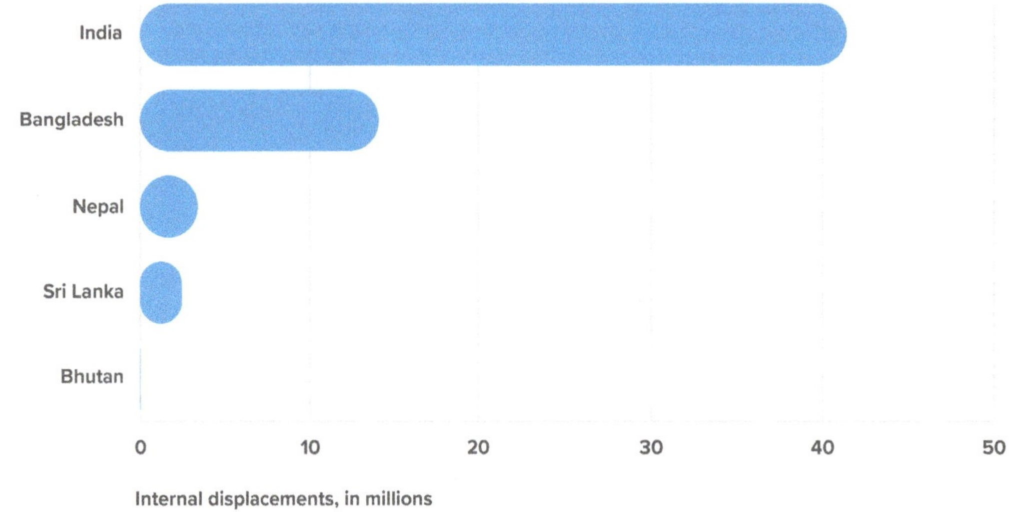

Figure 17: Five Countries and Territories with the most Disaster Displacements in South Asia (2010–2021)

Source: Internal Displacement Monitoring Centre, 2022

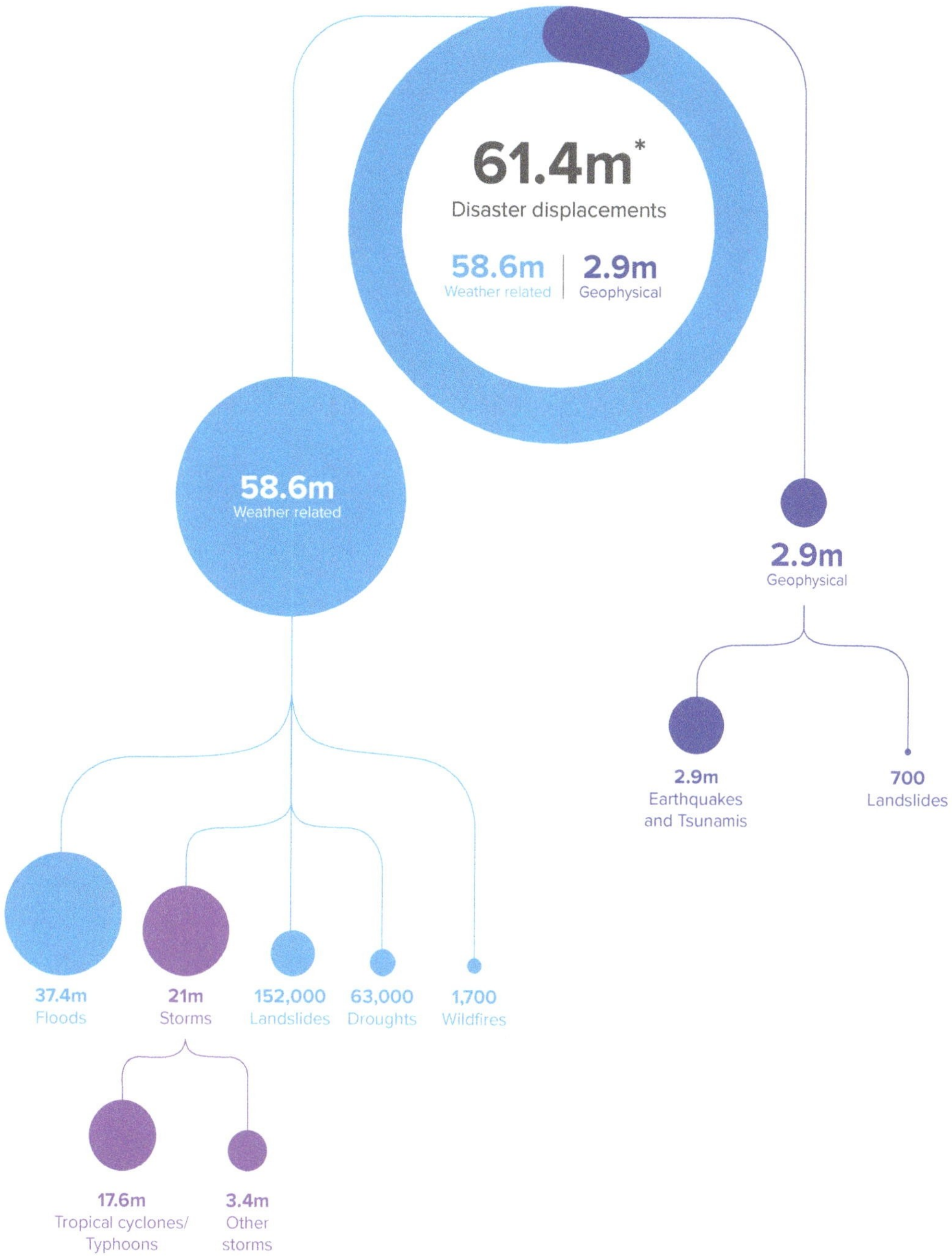

Figure 18: Disaster Displacements in South Asia: Breakdown by Hazard (2010–2021)

Source: Internal Displacement Monitoring Centre, 2022

8% of the regional total

Countries across Central and West Asia are confronted with a wide range of hazards including floods and flash floods, storms, drought, and earthquakes. Climate change is expected to increase the likelihood of extreme weather events, especially droughts and glacier melt.[74] The subregion also faces the cascading impacts of disasters on water scarcity, food insecurity, and conflict, all of which fuel displacement risk.

During 2010–2021, disasters caused 17.9 million internal displacements, a figure that represents 8% of the total recorded in the broader Asia and Pacific region. Pakistan reported the highest figures, which were mostly the result of devastating floods that hit the country in 2010 (Figure 20). This single event was deemed the most severe disaster in the country since 1929.[75] This event, which triggered 11.2 million internal displacements, was an outlier among those recorded in the broader Asia and Pacific region that year. Afghanistan was also affected by floods, most notably in 2010 and 2018. The country is subject to climate extremes, and floods normally take place in the form of flash floods due to snowmelt and heavy rains during the spring months.[76]

Relative to their population, other Central Asian countries have been badly affected by floods, some of which have been driven by dam failures and collapses, as was the case in the Sardoba Reservoir Dam on the Uzbek side of the Syr Darya river in 2020.[77] Following a week of heavy rains in May, the 3-year-old dam burst and washed away more than 35,000 hectares of land in Uzbekistan and Kazakhstan. The flooding forced about 70,000 people out of their homes in Uzbekistan, and around 32,000 in the Kazakh region of Turkistan, a third of which was underwater.[78]

Countries in Central and West Asia are also challenged by the impacts of drought, but the data on displacement associated with this and other slow-onset hazards is difficult to come by (Figure 21). Some evidence is emerging, however, showing a trend. In Afghanistan, for example, years of successive dry spells and below-average rainfall led to drought conditions in 2018 that forced people to leave their homes as their livelihoods became unviable and their living conditions untenable.[79] The impacts continued in 2019 as poor harvests increased food insecurity across the country, leaving many IDPs in dire conditions of poverty and malnutrition.[80] In total, the 2018 drought caused more than 371,000 displacements.

In June 2021, the Government of Afghanistan declared another country-wide drought.[81] The disaster took place as foreign military forces were withdrawing from the country, and the Taliban was intensifying its offensives to re-take major cities, including Kabul. Evidence shows that conflict and disasters in Afghanistan are intertwined. Drought may be the final straw for families living in rural areas underserviced after years of armed conflict. Drought also drives food insecurity and water scarcity, heightening the needs of those affected by conflict—including IDPs—and may hamper their ability to achieve durable solutions despite a lull in conflict since August 2021.[82]

Water scarcity was also a major factor in fuelling cross-border clashes between the Kyrgyz Republic and Tajikistan that triggered displacement in 2021.[83] In the region more broadly, dam construction, unsustainable agriculture practices, and glacial melt further threaten water supplies.[84] Drought and other environmental factors are already affecting agriculture, which accounts for a significant part of the Central Asian economy.[85] Human mobility patterns are also shifting, particularly those of communities that rely on transhumance and pastoralism.[86]

Earthquakes have also triggered displacement in several countries across Central and West Asia, with the Republic of Türkiye being the hotspot. Due to its location where the Anatolian, Eurasian, African, and Arabian plates meet, more than 95% of the landmass of Türkiye is prone to earthquakes. An estimated 70% of its population and 75% of its industrial facilities are in areas considered to be at high earthquake risk.[87]

During 2010–2021, 11 earthquakes triggered more than 292,000 internal displacements in Türkiye.[88] The most significant event was a 7.2 magnitude earthquake in 2011 which led to 252,000 displacements in the eastern Van province. A series of aftershocks and another

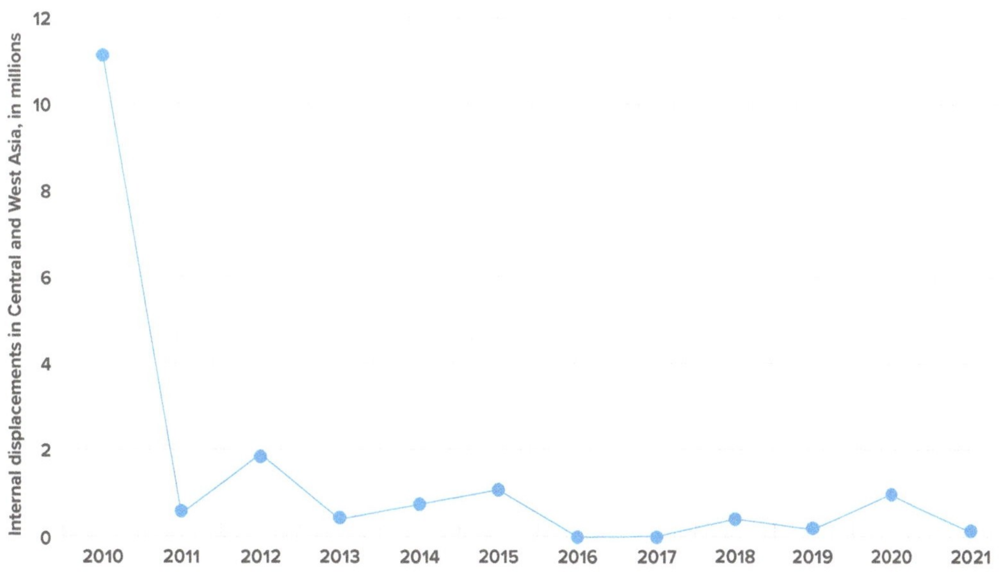

Figure 19: Internal Displacements by Disasters in Central and West Asia (2010–2021)

Source: Internal Displacement Monitoring Centre, 2022

5.6 magnitude earthquake followed less than 2 weeks later, all of which killed over 600 people and caused thousands of buildings to collapse. Aging and decaying infrastructure aggravated the seismic vulnerability of buildings and illustrated the need to strengthen disaster resilience, particularly in urban areas.[89]

Another powerful earthquake that hit the region took place in October 2015, when a 7.5 magnitude earthquake struck northern Afghanistan, triggering an estimated 55,000 internal displacements.[90] Pakistan suffered the brunt of the impact, with 666,000 displacements and 29,000 homes destroyed in Khyber Pakhtunkhwa, the former Federally Administered Tribal Areas.[91] In May 2012, several earthquakes and aftershocks triggered 36,000 displacements in Azerbaijan and 6,000 in Tajikistan. In Azerbaijan, an assessment carried out on more than 5,000 buildings estimated that nearly 2,000 were rendered unhabitable, which prolonged the displacement of people.[92]

Countries in the subregion are likely to face a growing risk of disaster displacement, notably by floods and slow-onset hazards such as droughts, desertification, and glacier melt. It is projected that increasing temperatures—combined with evaporation and glacial melt—will put the dry lands of Central and West Asia under increasing stress. Some parts of the subregion will face reduced water supply while others will have to cope with greater flood risk. Geophysical hazards may continue to pose a threat, which underscores the need to build more resilient infrastructure.[93]

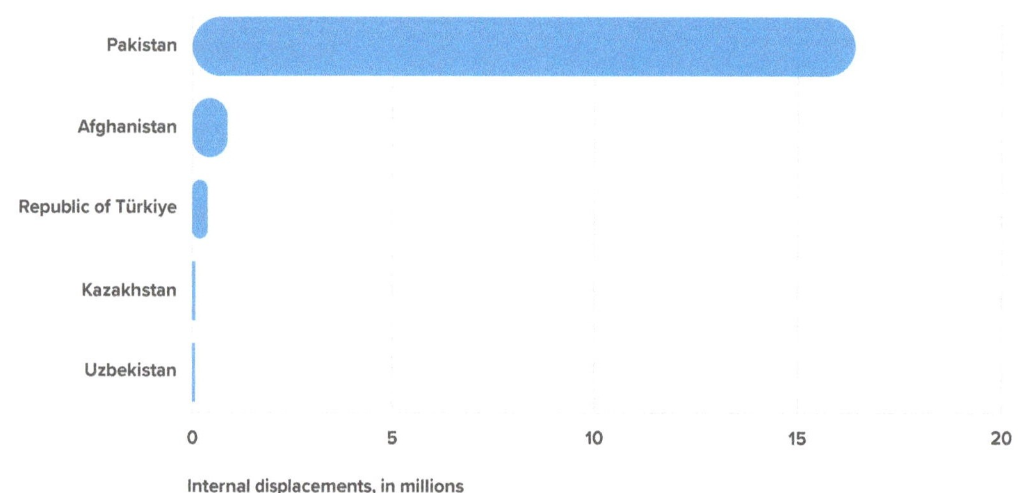

Figure 20: Five Countries and Territories with the most Disaster Displacements in Central and West Asia (2010–2021) Source: Internal Displacement Monitoring Centre, 2022

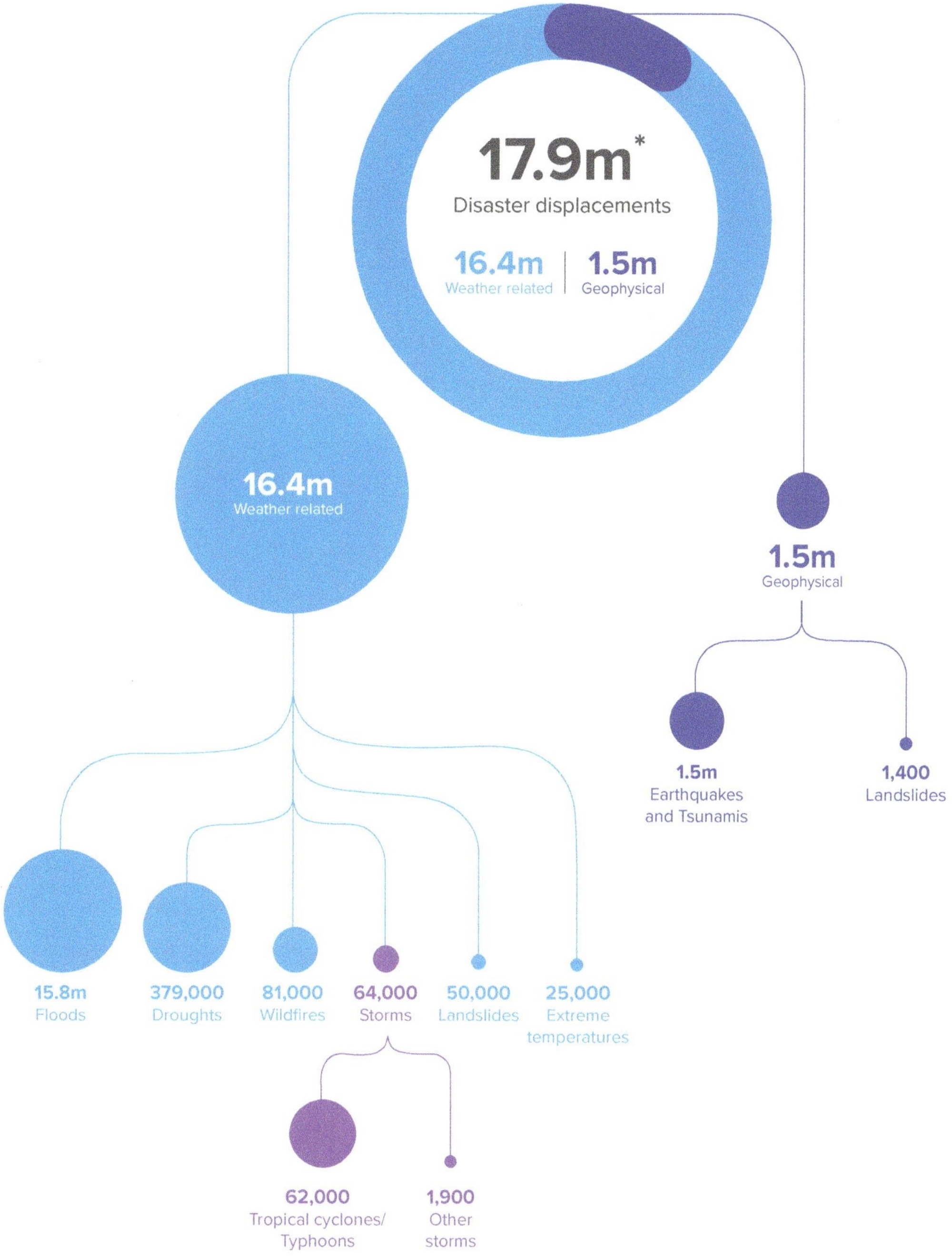

Figure 21: Disaster Displacements in Central and West Asia: Breakdown by Hazard (2010–2021)

Source: Internal Displacement Monitoring Centre, 2022

The Pacific

0.4% of the regional total

Thousands of people are forced to flee their homes in the Pacific every year due to the devastating impacts of sudden and slow-onset disasters. Small island states bear the greatest displacement risk relative to their population size. Climate change combined with vulnerability, exposed infrastructure, and housing poses an existential threat for some Pacific islands that could see their populations move not only internally but also across borders.[94]

This is the case in Kiribati, for example, where a 1-meter sea-level rise could inundate two-thirds of the country, forcing communities to move.[95] Solomon Islands, Tonga, and Vanuatu are also ranked as the three most vulnerable countries to the effects of disasters and climate change globally, and other countries including Fiji, Papua New Guinea, and Timor-Leste also rank highly.[96] These countries are also affected by disaster displacement every year (Figure 23).

The Pacific only has 0.4% of the disaster displacements reported in the total Asia and Pacific region. Although this may seem low, the population of countries in this subregion is smaller compared to others in the region. In addition, Pacific island states are also experiencing high levels of urbanization, which has certain characteristics and challenges that require tailored policies to address and reduce disaster displacement risk.[97]

During 2010–2021, 914,000 internal displacements were recorded in the Pacific, more than half of which were caused by storms, including tropical cyclones (Figure 24). The South Pacific tropical cyclone season—from November to April—brings on average four to six tropical cyclones annually.[98] Tropical cyclones wreak havoc on coastal communities causing 80% of displacements to happen during these 6 months and triggering flooding and landslides that force inland communities to flee.

The remoteness of many small island developing states also has implications for their economies, and for managing large-scale disasters that require an international response. This was the case, for example, when tropical cyclone Harold hit several countries in April 2020. This cyclone triggered the highest number of disaster displacements in the Pacific during 2010–2021, with more than 93,000 recorded across Fiji, Solomon Islands, Tonga, and Vanuatu. As the countries were already struggling to cope with the spread of the coronavirus disease (COVID-19) pandemic, measures to contain the virus hampered humanitarian interventions, and overseas aid workers were not allowed to enter. Despite the challenges in responding, the situation led to innovative ways of strengthening local capacities and systems. Local volunteers were trained online, and other countries and international agencies provided the authorities with remote support.[99]

The natural cycles of the El Niño and La Niña climatic periods increase the severity and frequency of extreme weather events in the Pacific region. For example, a strong manifestation of La Niña in 2012 contributed to some of the worst floods reported in the region, triggering about 99,000 internal displacements across Australia, Fiji, Papua

Coping with the effects of climate change. Family affected by recurring droughts, heavy rains and weather-related hazards in Timor-Leste. The increased frequency and intensity of disasters in a context of climate change are key drivers of displacement. (Photo by IFRC/SamSmith)

New Guinea, and Solomon Islands. 71,000 were recorded in Papua New Guinea alone, as heavy seasonal rains resulted in widespread flooding and landslides across eight provinces.[100]

The impacts of weather extremes on displacement are also visible in higher-income countries, including Australia and New Zealand.[101] Australia has experienced the compounding impacts of high-intensity wildfires followed by devastating floods. Wildfires fueled by climate change triggered close to 65,000 internal displacements across the country between July 2019 and February 2020 and burned an area the size of the United Kingdom.[102] A little over a year later, the worst-hit states of New South Wales and Victoria experienced widespread flooding, forcing 40,000 people out of their homes.[103] As climate change increases the severity and frequency of both hazards, the possibility of them striking simultaneously or in closer succession will grow, likely driving new and secondary displacement.[104]

Located on the Pacific Ring of Fire, several small island states have experienced earthquakes, tsunamis, and volcanic eruptions that have caused approximately 122,000 internal displacements during 2010–2021. A 7.5 magnitude earthquake in the Southern Highlands province of Papua New Guinea in 2018 caused the most significant displacement event, forcing 58,000 people from their homes. Due to the remoteness of many of the areas affected, some IDPs were still in need of assistance months after the disaster.[105]

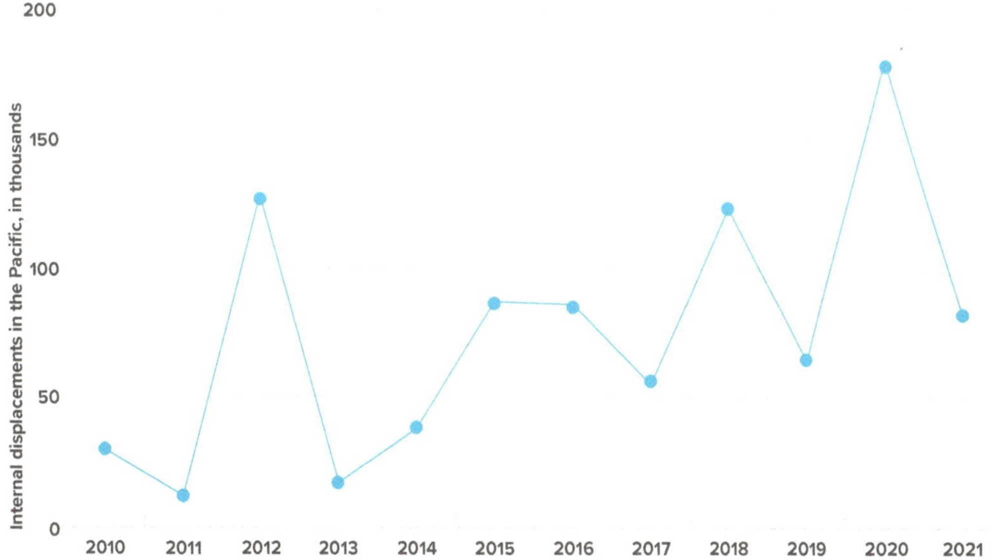

Figure 22: Internal Displacements by Disasters in the Pacific (2010–2021)

Source: Internal Displacement Monitoring Centre, 2022

With about half their population living within 10 km of the coast, Pacific small island states are at risk of slow-onset events such as coastal erosion, saline intrusion, and sea-level rise, all of which have the potential to cause severe economic and human impacts.[106] Under the latest predictions from the Intergovernmental Panel on Climate Change (IPCC), sea-level rise, salt water intrusion, and coastal flooding will threaten the livelihoods of coastal communities.[107] Permanent relocation as an adaptation to slow-onset disasters is sometimes the only solution for communities living on low-lying islands.[108]

Communities from the Carterets Islands in Papua New Guinea have already faced pressure to relocate. Since 1994, islanders from the seven atolls forming the Carteret Islands—which lie only 1.2 m above sea level—have already lost about 50% of their land.[109] Portrayed as the world's first "environmental migrants," several families have been relocated to Bougainville Island around 80 km away.[110] Resettlement programs are being led by the government and the community to continue their relocation and integration with host communities.[111]

Pacific islanders may also choose not to leave following disasters. Factors influencing this decision include cultural, historical, and spiritual attachments to land and political considerations such as self-determination. Pacific Island states' climate response plans and relocation policies, therefore, consider planned relocation as an option of last resort and provide support to those who wish to stay.[112] Examples of populations resisting relocation in preference to remaining in place are emerging. This is the case of the low-lying community of Togoru in Fiji, which chose to remain and adapt in situ despite facing severe coastal impacts.[113]

Small island states in the Pacific have demonstrated high levels of resilience and leadership on the issues of displacement and planned relocation. Lessons learned have been translated into policies and best practices for countries like Fiji and Vanuatu, while others are following suit. The role of indigenous knowledge will remain essential in supporting the resilience of communities exposed to disasters and the effects of climate change in the Pacific.[114] Regional collaboration will be key to addressing common national challenges linked to internal displacement, paving the way for more sustainable development.

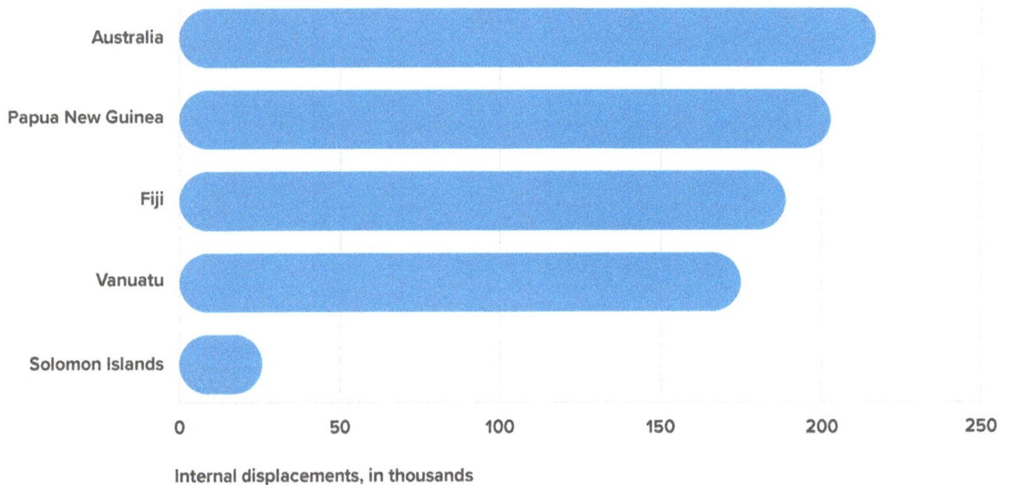

Figure 23: Five Countries and Territories with the most Disaster Displacements in the Pacific (2010–2021)

Source: Internal Displacement Monitoring Centre, 2022

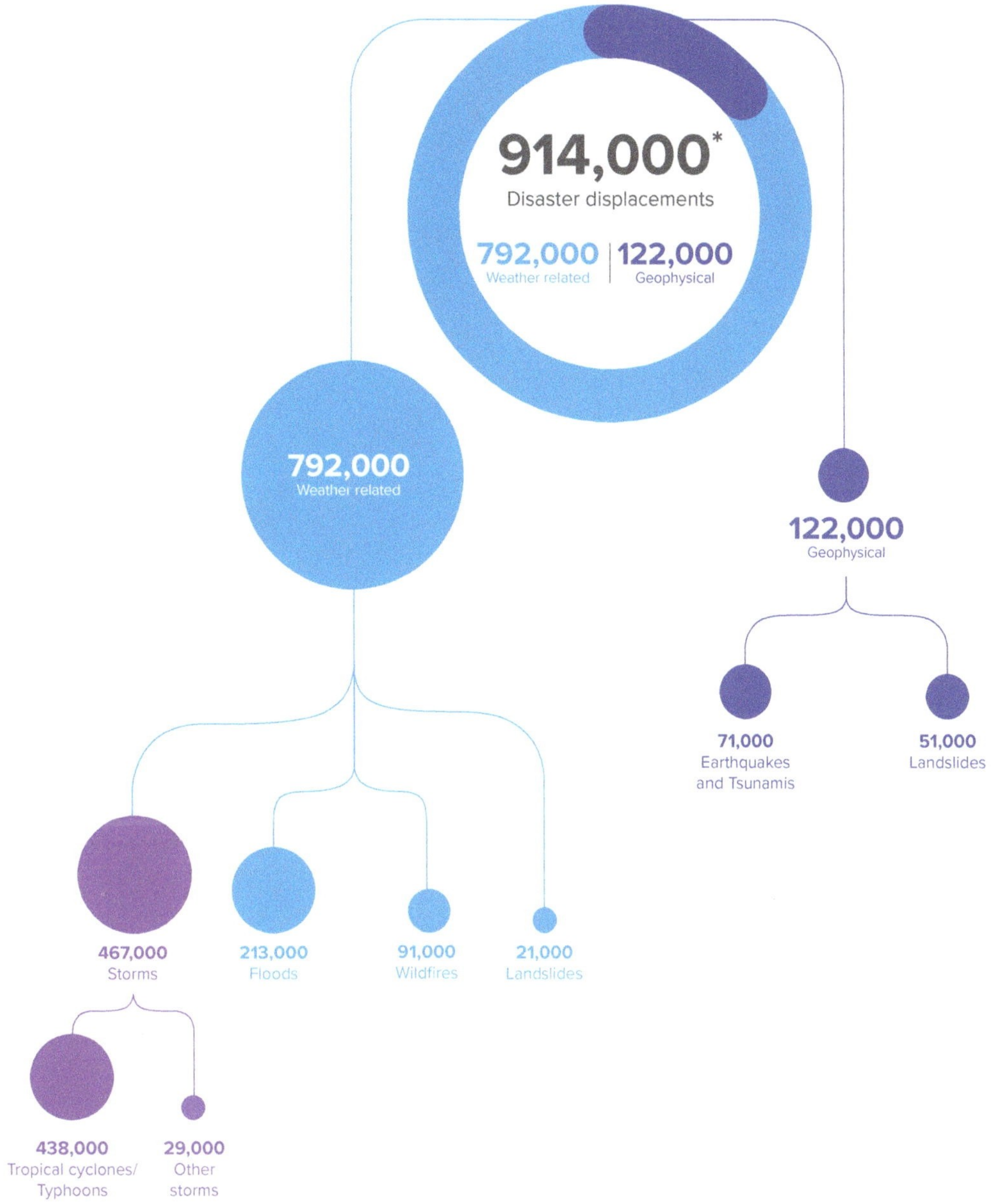

Figure 24: Disaster Displacements in the Pacific: Breakdown by Hazard (2010–2021)

Source: Internal Displacement Monitoring Centre, 2022

Part 2

Measuring the Social and Economic Impacts of Disaster Displacement in Asia and the Pacific

Facing destruction. An elderly survivor of the floods contemplates his destroyed home in Pakistan. (Photo by Asian Development Bank)

Short- and Long-term Economic Impacts

Annual economic losses caused by disasters in the Asia and Pacific region are estimated to be around $780 billion as of 2021, which is the equivalent of 2.5% of the regional gross domestic product (GDP). In the worst climate change scenario, these losses will increase to $1.4 trillion by 2059, and will disproportionally affect the economies of the Pacific small island states.[115] Relative to country GDPs, economic losses in the region are higher than in the rest of the world, and the gap has been widening.[116,117]

However, the cost of damage to housing and infrastructure is only a part of the equation. Displacement caused by disasters has further financial repercussions that have not been properly assessed. Displaced people often lose their land and property, while their ability to earn a living and contribute to the economy may be compromised. Displacement also creates needs that have to be paid for by IDPs themselves, host communities, governments, or aid providers. In the case of large-scale, protracted displacement, these consequences can hinder the development of entire societies.[118] While every country around the world can be affected by disaster displacement, lower-income countries suffer the most from its economic consequences that can amount to a significant proportion of their GDP.

Accounting for these impacts in a region where disasters are as frequent and severe as in Asia and the Pacific shows that relying on emergency response is unsustainable and that the only way forward is to invest in the prevention of disaster displacement. Each time a person is displaced, costs arise. After the Central Sulawesi earthquake in Indonesia in 2018, humanitarian organizations requested $15.6 million to provide emergency shelter—including tents and tarpaulins, and non-food items—to 62,500 people, a cost of nearly $250 per person.[119] They requested a further $6 million for camp coordination and management, and to transport IDPs to areas where they could access basic services.[120] Even in the case of short-term displacement, costs for people and economies can be significant (Spotlight: Flood-related Displacement in Jakarta, Indonesia).

Displaced family in Indonesia. A displaced woman and her child at an emergency camp in Palu, in Indonesia's Central Sulawesi, after an earthquake and tsunami hit the area on September 28, 2018. (Photo by JEWEL SAMAD/AFP via Getty Images)

Spotlight: Flood-related Displacement in Jakarta, Indonesia

Preventing, planning for, and responding to flood displacement is a priority for Indonesia, as one in four Indonesians lives in an area at high risk of flooding.[a] Many efforts have been made in this direction in Jakarta. Local authorities and non-governmental organizations keep stocks of food, blankets, clothes, and medicine so that they are ready to provide support when floods come, and they often do.

In a study conducted by the Internal Displacement Monitoring Centre in 2022, over half of the people who had to leave their homes in Jakarta in 2021 had been displaced more than once.[b] Most of them found refuge in the same neighborhood and were displaced for less than a week. All were able to return home after their displacement.

Although affected people did return home after a few days, it was not without a cost. One in four respondents said they had to pay to repair their home, spending on average Rp1.6 million before they could return, the equivalent of over a month of their average income. In addition to this cost, they also faced losses. Many were unable to work for several days as floods prevented them from reaching their workplace and then forced them to stay home to clean and repair.

The financial costs and losses of disaster displacement weigh disproportionately on those with fewer resources. The people who are most often displaced are those forced to live in lower-quality houses near the riverbank, where rent is cheaper as a result of the recurring threat. Most work at lower-earning jobs as street peddlers, manual laborers, motorcycle taxi drivers, and housemaids. The average monthly income for displaced respondents was around Rp1.2 million compared with Rp3.7 million for non-displaced respondents.

As a result, they were highly dependent on aid and help from their families and friends during their displacement. About 40% of respondents received some material or financial support from their family in Jakarta, 21% from the local government, and 19% from friends in Jakarta. About 4% received help from the national government or other organizations, including non-governmental organizations and international agencies.

Many studies on the cost of disasters in Indonesia have been published, but none have included the specific economic impacts of displacement.[c] Understanding these impacts on livelihoods, housing conditions, social networks, health, security, and education is key to further improving disaster response, recovery, and solutions to displacement.

Sources:

a J. Rentschler et al. 2021. Floods in the neighborhood: Mapping poverty and flood risk in Indonesian cities. World Bank Blog. 4 April; IDMC. Country Profile Indonesia (accessed 30 June 2022).

b IDMC. Country Profile Indonesia (accessed 30 June 2022).

c UNDRR. 2020. Disaster Risk Reduction in The Republic of Indonesia: Status Report 2020.; United Nations Development Programme, Indonesia. 2014. Institutionalizing Post-Disaster Recovery: Learning from Mentawai Tsunami and Merapi Eruption; Government of Indonesia. 2018. Impact of the Lombok Earthquake: 436 Died and Economic Losses of More than IDR 5.04 trillion. Jakarta; World Bank. 2021. Indonesia - Disaster Risk Finance and Insurance.

Tidal Floods in Jakarta, Indonesia. The effects of climate change, combined with high tide, led to devastating floods in North Jakarta, Indonesia, in November 2020. (Photo by Ahmad Rajif Sidiq/INA Photo Agency/Universal Images Group via Getty Images)

During the 2019–2020 Black Summer bushfires in Australia, the loss of economic production as a result of a person missing just 1 day of work because of displacement was estimated to be about $510.[121] In a survey in the states of New South Wales and South Australia, 55% of the respondents who were displaced for more than a night said that leaving had prevented them from working as normal.[122] If each person missed 2 days of work, the loss would amount to more than $500,000. Previous bushfire recovery efforts suggest it can take people between 1 and 4 years to rebuild their homes.[123] Considering that the cost of covering the housing needs of people who lost their homes for a year was estimated to be as much as $52 million, it can be considered that the longer displacement takes place, the higher the economic losses will be.[124]

When displaced people are unable to return home and remain displaced for months, years, or even decades, economic impacts add up. As a result of the widespread damage left by the Great East Japan earthquake and tsunami, and the inability of displaced people to return and rebuild the local economy, Fukushima entered a phase of serious economic recession.[125] In Nepal, the 2015 earthquake also bore consequences that are still being felt in 2022 (Spotlight: 7 Years after the Gorkha Earthquake in Nepal).

IDMC estimated the cost of providing IDPs with support for housing, healthcare, education, and security—and accounting for their loss of income for 1 year of displacement—at $21 billion worldwide in 2021.[126] In the case of Afghanistan, IDMC estimated the economic impact per IDP at $301 in 2021, amounting to over $418 million for the 1.4 million people displaced by disasters. The economic impact per IDP in Myanmar was higher at about $546. The cost of covering the basic needs of the 1,400 people recorded to be displaced by disasters in Myanmar at the end of 2021 would amount to nearly $784,000.

The variation in the economic impact per IDP arises from differences in their level of needs and the cost of meeting them. The type of interventions required, operational capacity, and access constraints also affect associated costs. For instance, the cost of providing nutrition assistance to one affected person was $46 in Afghanistan, compared with $143 in Myanmar.[127]

These estimates are highly conservative. They do not account for the longer-term economic consequences of displacement on future income or health of IDPs, nor do they include financial impacts on host communities. Despite only uncovering a fraction of the hidden costs and losses associated with disaster displacement, these figures reveal the substantial additional burden it can place on already fragile economies and an overstretched humanitarian system.

High-income countries are not spared, but impacts are often most severe for lower-income countries with comparatively small GDPs. When Cyclone Pam hit Vanuatu in 2015, it was estimated that just the cost of the damage caused by the cyclone already equated to 64% of the GDP.[128] Some 65,000 internal displacements were recorded during the disaster.[129] Had the additional costs and losses associated with these displacements been included, the estimated economic impact of the disaster would have been far greater.

Given the frequency and severity of disasters in the Asia and Pacific region, relying on emergency humanitarian responses to address internal displacement will become increasingly unsustainable. Taking pre-emptive action by building community resilience and investing in climate mitigation strategies, disaster risk reduction, and early warning systems could prove to be far less costly in the long term. Globally, disaster risk reduction interventions have an estimated return of four to seven times, which reinforces the economic value of acting early.[130]

Risk models can provide useful insights into understanding the potential costs associated with future displacement and help governments plan for them. While existing data is insufficient to provide detailed and comprehensive estimates, it is projected that 9.5 million people on average could be displaced by storm surges, riverine floods, earthquakes, cyclonic winds, and tsunamis in the Asia and Pacific region in any given year in the future. If every one of them is unable to earn their income for only 1 day, with an average daily GDP per capita of $29 across the region, the loss would already amount to $275.5 million.

Any calculations overlook current and future displacement linked with slow-onset disasters and climate change, as these are hardly ever recorded quantitatively at the global level. Desertification, glacial retreat, increasing temperatures, land and forest degradation, loss of biodiversity, ocean acidification, salinization, and sea-level rise do, however, force people to leave their homes as they lose territory, livelihoods, food or water, or face an ever-increasing risk of disasters.[131] Pacific small island states are already experiencing this type of displacement and its impacts on people and economies (Spotlight: "People used to live where the sea is now" in Papua New Guinea).

Disaster displacement creates many challenges for affected people and their governments. An improved understanding of the ways it affects their lives—but also local economies, infrastructure, and services—can help authorities design better programs to mitigate negative consequences and even seize potential opportunities. The arrival of IDPs can—if adequately managed and prepared—create economic growth in host areas. Conversely, if unaddressed, disaster displacement can jeopardize progress toward sustainable development goals and widen socioeconomic disparities, with those most vulnerable pushed even further behind.[132]

Spotlight: 7 Years after the Gorkha Earthquake in Nepal

The 2015 Gorkha earthquake in Nepal caused 2.6 million displacements and widespread damage and destruction in the capital, Kathmandu, which was near the epicenter.[a] The lost economic production caused by internally displaced people (IDPs) being unable to carry out their usual economic activities while displaced was estimated at around $406 million.[b] At the end of 2021, thousands of people were still displaced. In the immediate aftermath of the event, support from the government, and national and international organizations took many forms. They set up temporary shelters and cash-for-work programs and distributed food, emergency items, and cash.

A study conducted in the Sindhupalchok District in 2022 found that costs were also borne by displaced and non-displaced people in host areas.[c] Non-displaced respondents (44%) reported additional expenses after the arrival of IDPs, in particular, increased utility bills; higher prices for food, goods, furniture, or rent; and the costs of buying food and supplies for the IDPs.

The government granted displaced families NRs300,000 to rebuild their houses about a year after the earthquake, but the cost of rebuilding was often more than that. At the time of the study, some IDPs remained in their first temporary shelters where they were exposed to heat in the summer and cold in the winter.

Lack of income is the main issue for IDPs, even in 2022. Livelihood opportunities were limited for everyone after the earthquake, but IDPs experienced more severe impacts. Displaced respondents (22%) lost their entire income in 2015, and 64% of them were still unemployed 7 years later. By comparison, 12% of non-displaced respondents lost their income in 2015 and 50% of them were still unemployed at the time of the survey. Those working in 2022 earned on average NRs28,704 per month for displaced households, compared with NRs48,553 for non-displaced households.

Many IDPs work in the informal sector or as daily laborers, with women doing work at home and men working in mines and construction. Some members of the host community work in similar conditions, but more of them own farmland nearby or have a small business that allows for higher earnings. Owners of businesses and land have benefited to some extent from the arrival of IDPs in the area, as this has led to an increase in prices.

Lower employment rates and income for IDPs can also be linked to their lower educational levels, a barrier that is likely to endure for the next generation. Many children had their education interrupted after the earthquake as schools had to be repaired and rebuilt, but displaced children were more affected. Displaced children (85%) experienced a break in their schooling, 66% of them for 1–6 months, and 17% for more than a year. That compares to 80% of non-displaced children experiencing a break in their education, 81% for 1–6 months, and 7% for more than a year. Nearly all the children in both groups eventually returned to school.

The difference may be explained by the fact that the financial difficulties faced by displaced families kept their children out of school for longer periods. Some children had to work to help their families. Some of them also reportedly stayed out of school because they were traumatized by the disaster, while others faced language barriers.

The 2015 Gorkha earthquake affected everyone in the Kathmandu area, but IDPs experienced these effects more. Despite a wide range of aid mechanisms—including in-kind assistance and financial support from the Government of Nepal and non-governmental organizations—some of these effects are still being felt 7 years later.

NRs = Nepalese rupees

Sources:

a Disaster Risk Management Knowledge Centre. Country Risk Profile (accessed 29 June 2022).

b IDMC. 2018. Lost production due to internal displacement: The 2015 earthquake in Nepal.

c IDMC. Country Profile Nepal (accessed 28 June 2022).

Displacement camp in the Gorkha district, Nepal. Following the 2015 earthquake, hundreds of displaced people faced a harsh winter at high altitudes in their temporary shelters. (Photo by © UNICEF/ UN017137/Shrestha)

Spotlight: "People used to live where the sea is now" in Papua New Guinea

Papua New Guinea (PNG) is highly vulnerable to the impacts of climate change including increasing temperatures, acidification, salinization, and sea-level rise.[a] PNG is more vulnerable to sea-level rise than the global average, and coastal erosion has already caused internal displacement.[b] The Carteret islands were among the first documented cases worldwide of displacement caused by the phenomenon. Tens of thousands of PNG inhabitants could face permanent inundation by 2070 to 2100.[c]

As the slow-onset effects of climate change, the related disasters, displacements, and economic impacts are expected to increase in the coming years, understanding their causes and consequences better is essential for planning, prevention, and preparedness. Yet, data on how displacement in the context of climate change affects lives and leads to financial costs and losses are largely lacking.

As a contribution to fill this knowledge gap, the Internal Displacement Monitoring Centre conducted a study in 2022 near Port Moresby, the capital and largest city of PNG.[d] In 2018 and 2019, they interviewed 150 people who had to leave their homes because of sea-level rise or related disasters, including coastal erosion, inundation, and salination.

The study highlighted some of the reasons why monitoring this type of displacement is challenging. The first is that displacement linked with slow-onset events happens gradually, rather than in one massive movement. People started to move from "where the sea is now" in the early 2000s. Initially, only a few people moved, then entire families, with a significant increase since 2016.

The second reason is that affected people themselves may not link their displacement to climate change. In this case, sea-level rise over the past decades had led to increased flooding, coastal erosion, and the deterioration of water quality in the area. The gradual reduction of land available for people to live on and off resulted in overcrowding, which several respondents mentioned as a reason for moving elsewhere, rather than sea-level rise.

The third reason is that the impacts of this type of displacement are less visible and immediate than those of more sudden and drastic changes. Most of the displaced respondents resettled close to where they used to live but further inland, on land they already owned and previously used for subsistence farming. After some time, they rebuilt homes of similar standards to the ones they used to live in. They rely on the same health and educational facilities they used to in the nearby town.

That is not to say, however, that displacement had no impact. Displaced respondents (17%) lost their income entirely upon their displacement, and 88% of them remained without income for more than 1 year. Years later in 2022, 4% live in a collective shelter and 3% in a makeshift shelter or the open air. Others (6%) are hosted by someone else, with no home of their own. The average value of the displaced respondents' homes is lower, at about K19,000 compared to K26,000 for non-displaced respondents.

When displacement is unrecorded, it receives less attention, and affected people receive less support from the authorities and aid providers. The costs of its impacts are mostly borne by displaced people themselves, their host communities, and their families. One-third of the non-displaced respondents share their home with at least one displaced person, mostly members of their own family. One-quarter of the non-displaced respondents reported having to face additional expenses since the arrival of displaced people in the area, noting an increase in the price of food, goods, and utilities, as well as the support they provide to displaced people who share their home. About one-quarter of the displaced respondents and one-third of the non-displaced respondents reported receiving financial support from family or friends, for the same average amount of K225 per month.

The arrival of displaced people led to an increase in population density but it was not followed by corresponding investments in local infrastructure, services, and livelihood opportunities to cover the needs of everyone. One-third of the displaced and non-displaced respondents reported that they have less access to healthcare in 2022 compared to before displacement, which can be the result of overcrowding in nearby health facilities.

As the scale of displacement is caused by slow-onset disasters, the impacts can be difficult to identify and measure. Collecting more information on this rising phenomenon is necessary to provide adequate support and to inform plans to prevent and respond to future displacement in the context of climate change.

K = Papua New Guinea Kina

Sources:

a World Bank. 2021. Climate Risk Country Profile: Papua New Guinea.

b WBG Climate Change Knowledge Portal (CCKP) 2021. Papua New Guinea Climate Data: Projections.

c Government of the UK, Met Office. 2014. Human dynamics of climate change: Technical Report. London.

d IDMC. Country Profile Papua New Guinea (accessed 30 June 2022).

At risk of displacement. A coastal community in Papua New Guinea, where the main source of livelihood is fishing. People depending on the sea for their income and food are highly vulnerable to the effects of climate change and related displacement. (Photo by the Asian Development Bank)

Differentiated Impacts of Disaster Displacement

Each person experiences displacement differently: men and women, boys and girls, and people of various abilities and identities face different risks and can contribute to solutions in their way. Displacement tends to exacerbate pre-existing vulnerabilities and reinforce social inequalities. Poorer households, for instance, are often disproportionately affected in a disaster, as documented in India.[133] Understanding these specificities is essential to designing inclusive and effective support, as illustrated in the case of displacement linked with volcanic eruptions in Vanuatu (Spotlight: Differentiated Impacts of Displacement in Vanuatu).

Children and Youth

Children and youth face particular threats in displacement, which puts their security, wellbeing, and future at risk.[134] Living conditions in collective shelters—including overcrowding and lack of access to clean water and sanitation—can facilitate the spread of communicable or vector-borne diseases to which children are especially vulnerable. Disruptions in the habits of children—including interruptions in their education—can be very harmful to their stability and psychosocial development.

Displacement tends to interrupt education at least for a few days, but often for several months, and sometimes for years. Distance from school and lack of transportation from the place of refuge, insecurity or lack of financial resources to pay for fees, uniforms, or books, are the most frequent barriers to education, with potential repercussions throughout the current and future lives of displaced children and young people.[135]

Elderly People

At the other end of the life cycle, older people also face distinct challenges. They may be left behind in disasters, particularly if they have a disability. Following severe floods in Pakistan, as much as 10% of the older population was found living without family support after their relatives had fled the disaster and left them behind.[136]

The elderly may also have difficulties accessing food distribution or may be unable to eat it if it is not adapted to their needs.[137] Makeshift shelters where older IDPs have to sleep on hard or damp surfaces can lead to chronic joint pain becoming acute and debilitating when it was manageable before displacement.[138] Social isolation can place an additional burden on their mental health and cause high levels of depression, as seen after the 1999 earthquake in Taipei,China.[139]

Gender and Sexual Orientation

Displacement also increases gender disparities, and displaced women and girls are often at higher risk of neglect, abuse, and violence than their non-displaced counterparts or displaced men and boys.[140] Poor housing conditions that offer no barriers against assaults, separation from social networks and known environments, and destitution can make displaced women and girls more vulnerable to sexual and gender-based violence, as reported for instance in the context of cyclone Winston in Fiji.[141]

Internally displaced women are also at higher risk of intimate partner violence, as was documented after cyclones and tsunamis in Bangladesh and Sri Lanka.[142] The mental health and sense of security of women are often more impacted than men in displacement. Near Kathmandu, Nepal, 7 years after the Gorkha earthquake, a third of the displaced women reported feeling worried, nervous, angry, or sad more often now than before their displacement, compared to 23% of the displaced men. Those who were displaced multiple times after the event, and those who had a disability were even more affected.[143]

IDPs who identify as lesbian, gay, bisexual, transgender/transsexual, intersex queer/questioning, and other gender non-conforming people (LGBTIQ+) also face multiple risks of violence and exclusion.[144] In Pakistan, following the 2011 floods, hijaras—who are generally assigned male at birth but could also include intersex people—were excluded from aid for appearing not to match the sex listed on their ID.[145]

Similar experiences have been noted among the Aravanis of India, who consider themselves neither men nor women.[146] In addition, some choose not to access aid due to fears of repercussions. In Fiji, some lesbian and transgender people stayed in private residences or safe houses rather than public evacuation centers when tropical cyclone Winston hit.[147] The waria (male-to-female transgender people in Indonesia) made a similar decision after the eruption of Mount Merapi in Indonesia in 2010.[148]

People with Disabilities

It is estimated that about 690 million people in the Asia and Pacific region are living with a disability, including those with physical or cognitive disabilities, those who are blind or experience low vision, and those with multiple disabilities, amongst others.[149] Inadequate housing and higher rates of poverty among people with disabilities can heighten the exposure and vulnerability of IDPs with disabilities to slow- and sudden-onset hazards, increasing their risk of displacement.[150]

Disaster risk reduction measures, early warning systems, and evacuation shelters are too often inaccessible for people with disabilities, heightening their risk of being injured or separated from carers or assistive devices. In an assessment after Cyclone Amphan hit Bangladesh in 2020, the majority of the people with hearing difficulties said they could not hear the cyclone preparedness warnings delivered over the microphone.[151]

Those who do manage to reach safety often face discrimination and intersecting barriers to accessing housing, livelihoods, healthcare, and education, which can hinder their ability to find durable solutions.[152] A survey after flooding on the eastern coast of Australia in 2017 found that people with disabilities and their carers were more likely to have been displaced for 6 months longer than people without disabilities, and experienced greater disruptions to their access to food, support networks, and essential services.[153] A lack of affordable temporary accommodation meant many had to live in unsafe accommodation, relocate to other areas, or became homeless.[154] Despite these ongoing challenges, some progress has been made in ensuring planning and responses to disaster displacement are more inclusive of people with disabilities (Box 1).

Spotlight: Differentiated Impacts of Displacement in Vanuatu

There is growing evidence that women, children, indigenous people, and those with disabilities are particularly affected by the negative impacts of disaster displacement in Vanuatu.[a] To better understand these differentiated impacts, the Internal Displacement Monitoring Centre conducted a study on displacement linked with the Manaro Voui volcanic eruptions on Ambae island in December 2021. The increased volcanic activity led to two compulsory evacuations of the entire population of the island in 2017 and 2018.[b] The majority of residents had returned to Ambae by November 2019, but 2,300 were still residing in displacement sites across different islands, including 1,700 on Espiritu Santo (Santo).[c]

Of the 154 internally displaced people (IDPs) surveyed on Santo, most IDPs faced disruptions to their livelihoods as a result of displacement, but women appeared to be particularly affected. Of the displaced women, 33% became unemployed as a result of their displacement, compared with 20% of the men. Women also remained unemployed for longer than men.

Overall about 41% of the displaced women and 67% of the men the men earn money from work on Santo. Women tend to look after their families more, while men often earn money by gardening and selling kava and other produce at local markets. Some also work in shops, construction, or other forms of daily labor. Gender disparities in access to work seemed to be less pronounced amongst non-displaced respondents, with 54% of non-displaced women working, compared with 58% of men.

Gender disparities were also found amongst displaced children. The majority of boys and girls from displaced households experienced breaks in their schooling because of displacement, but girls tended to be out of school for a longer period. Most attend school on Santo, but the enrolment rate is slightly lower amongst girls (86%) than boys (92%). When asked why they do not send their daughters to school, some parents said they were already married or needed to work. In contrast, the enrolment rate is the same for girls and boys from non-displaced households.

In addition to the impacts on women and girls, the study also highlighted some of the unique challenges people with disabilities faced during displacement. Of surveyed IDPs, 5% were identified as having a disability. According to key respondents, limited space on the ships and flights used to transport evacuees meant many people with disabilities were forced to leave behind their assistance devices or were separated from their carers.

Upon arriving on Santo, about 200 evacuees with disabilities were temporarily housed in a shipping terminal on Santo wharf, where they had no privacy, limited access to sanitation facilities, and many slept on the ground.[d] Organizations of people with disabilities and non-governmental organizations made efforts to address these barriers.[e] Despite this, IDPs with disabilities continued to encounter challenges accessing clean water, toilets, and work during their displacement. Most said they had not been consulted about how assistance provided could be adapted to their needs.

Such findings highlight how the needs and experiences of people during displacement can vary depending on their sex, age, and disability status. Expanding the collection of disaggregated data on IDPs can assist in understanding these differences and fostering more inclusive planning and responses.

Sources:

a See e.g., RNZ. 2018. Efforts to restore sense of routine for Ambae children. 21 August; World Vision. 2019. Tropical Cyclone Harold: Three months on; Care. 2015. Rapid Gender Analysis Cyclone Pam Vanuatu. 7 April; Minority Rights. 2019. Vanuatu: Indigenous language loss and the multiplying effects of climate change.

b Shelter Cluster for Vanuatu. 2017. Ambae Mass Evacuation 2017

Response Review; Shelter Cluster for Vanuatu. 2018. Vanuatu Ambae Volcano 2018.

c IOM DTM. 2019. Vanuatu - Ambae Evacuee Response, Returns Report - Round 6 (November 2019).

d Daily Post VU. 2018. No more sleeping on the floor, 17 September.

e See e.g. Field Ready. 2018. Responding to Volcano Ambae in Vanuatu. 6 September.

Volcanic activity in Vanuatu. An adolescent girl evacuated to Santo with her family as a result of volcanic activity on the island of Ambae. (Photo by © UNICEF/UNI324718/Shing)

Box 1: Regional Progress towards Disability Inclusion in Displacement Planning and Responses

The Incheon Strategy to "Make the Right Real" for persons with disabilities in Asia and the Pacific 2013–2022 was the first set of regionally agreed disability-inclusive development targets.[a] It includes goals to strengthen disability-inclusive disaster risk reduction and implement measures to provide timely and appropriate support to people with disabilities affected by disasters.[b] Although the midpoint review of the strategy indicated that implementation had been slow, several promising practices have emerged in the region that point towards more inclusive preparedness and responses.[c]

In countries like Indonesia and Nepal, organizations of people with disabilities have been actively strengthening disaster risk management and improving the accessibility of emergency shelters and services.[d] A multi-year project in the Pacific Islands seeks to enhance the effectiveness and inclusiveness of regional early warning systems, including improved integration of people with disabilities.[e]

There is also growing recognition that more robust data on people with disabilities are essential to inform targeted planning.[f] Launched in the Philippines in 2018, the Inclusive Data Management System for Persons with Disabilities is a system for identifying people with disabilities and collecting data on their needs, vulnerabilities, and capacities before, during, and after disasters.[g] It aims to promote the inclusion of people with disabilities in planning, budgeting, and other development processes of local governments and agencies in disaster risk reduction and management.

As the Asia and Pacific region continues to be one of the regions most adversely affected by disasters, enhancing these efforts and ensuring people with disabilities play an active role in shaping climate adaptation strategies, disaster risk reduction measures, and responses to displacement are key to addressing displacement-related risks in the region and advancing a more inclusive future.

Sources:

a UNESCAP. 2018. Incheon Strategy.

b UNESCAP. 2018. Incheon Strategy.

c UNESCAP. 2017. Midpoint review of the implementation of the Incheon Strategy to "Make the Right Real" for Persons with Disabilities in Asia and the Pacific. E/ESCAP/APDDP(4)/1. 27 September.

d See e.g. GFDRR and World Bank Group. 2017. Disability Inclusion in Disaster Risk Management; National Federal of the Disabled – Nepal. N.D. Towards inclusion of persons with disabilities in Nepal – Phase II (accessed 17 August 2021).

e World Meteorological Organization. N.D. Strengthening Hydro-Meteorological and Early Warning Services in the Pacific (CREWS Pacific SIDS 2.0) (accessed 17 August 2021).

f UNGA. 2020. Panel discussion on promoting and protecting the rights of persons with disabilities in the context of climate change, Report of the Office of the United Nations High Commissioner for Human Rights, A/HRC/46/46. 22 December.

g Centre for Disaster Preparedness. 2021. Inclusive Data Management System Guidebook.

Indigenous People

The Asia and Pacific region is home to millions of indigenous people. Many depend on ecosystems that are particularly vulnerable to the effects of a changing climate and extreme weather events such as floods, droughts, heatwaves, wildfires, and cyclones.[155] When indigenous people are displaced to areas with different environmental conditions, they may lose their livelihoods, traditional knowledge, the spiritual connection they have with the land, and their languages and cultures.[156] The change in environment is often significant, particularly when indigenous communities leave rural homes for the cities.[157]

Indigenous communities are not only among the most affected by disaster displacement, but they can also play an active role in prevention, forecasting, and response. Their ancestral knowledge and in-depth understanding of their environment have long helped them prepare for and prevent disasters.[158] A greater understanding of the many ways in which disaster displacement disrupts the lives of different groups of people, creates new or heightened needs and threats, and adds to pre-existing vulnerabilities is essential for all to move toward a more inclusive and sustainable future in the Asia and Pacific region. Knowledge on this issue increases each year, but more research and better data are needed to give policymakers and aid providers the information they need to prevent, plan for and respond to disaster displacement more effectively.

Part 3

Understanding Displacement in Disaster Prevention, Response, and Recovery

Children in displacement. Thousands of children remained displaced for months or even years following the 2015 earthquake that hit the Gorkha district of Nepal. Protracted displacement can be especially harmful for children's health, education, security and psychosocial well-being. (Photo by © UNICEF/UN017146/Shrestha)

Pre-emptive Movements and the Importance of Resilience

Every year, millions of people across the Asia and Pacific region leave their homes in response to disaster alerts and early warning systems ahead of the impact of natural hazards. Although evacuations are a form of displacement, they are first and foremost a life-saving measure undertaken to avoid or mitigate the impacts of an anticipated hazard. Monitoring pre-emptive evacuations contributes to understanding its effectiveness as a risk reduction measure. Particular attention should be put on how people are protected in the event of being evacuated, including identifying their needs, preventing gender-based violence and exploitation, and making sure that those displaced take an active part in recovery programs.[159]

The success of both Bangladesh and India in limiting the loss of life through large-scale pre-emptive evacuations in the lead-up to cyclone Amphan in May 2020 is one such example. The governments pre-emptively evacuated 3.3 million people from densely populated and low-lying areas.[160] The risk-informed early warning systems and evacuation protocols of both countries were largely successful when compared to tropical cyclone Gorky, which hit the same areas in Bangladesh in 1991. This event—which was deemed one of the deadliest disasters in the 20th century—killed 139,000 people and left about 10 million displaced.[161]

The effectiveness of pre-emptive evacuations, however, depends on the responsiveness of people to evacuation orders, which in turn varies depending on the hazard and perceived risk. In 2018, when typhoon Jongdari approached Japan, only 4% of the people prompted to evacuate did so.[162] Those who stayed became trapped by landslides and rising floodwaters, and more than 170 people died, making Jongdari the deadliest weather-related disaster in Japan in decades. Several factors explained the reluctance of people to move—including age—but also the fact that in Japan evacuation orders are not mandatory.[163]

In addition, studies have found that the likelihood of following evacuation orders may vary between genders, given differences in exposure and risk perception.[164] A Facebook survey run during the Black Summer of 2019–2020 in Australia revealed that women were more likely to evacuate earlier than their male counterparts ahead of a bushfire.[165] Men, however, were more likely to return home sooner than the other members of their household.[166] Understanding how gender, age, and cultural backgrounds may shape the patterns of displacement is important, especially in such a diverse region.

Beyond government-led evacuations, people may also decide on their own to leave their homes before a disaster strikes. This form of pre-emptive displacement may have a similar protective value, but it is more difficult to monitor. Having data on voluntary and forced pre-emptive evacuations both inside and outside evacuation centers would help to draw lessons on disaster risk management and better understand displacement dynamics.

Except for a few countries in the region, there is an overall lack of disaggregated data and standardization on key concepts regarding pre-emptive movements ahead of disasters, making it impossible to understand how evacuations function as a risk reduction measure. Having such data would allow an understanding of the costs avoided by pre-emptively moving people from high-risk areas, which would bring insights into how different temporal dimensions of displacement can bring different financial implications to communities and countries.

The Role of Recovery and Reconstruction in Supporting Durable Solutions

Reporting on displacement in the Asia and Pacific region generally takes place during or after disasters hit. Most of this data comes from disaster damage and needs assessments that are produced by first responders a few days after disasters strike. In many instances, data collection takes place only once, leaving gaps in understanding of the duration of displacement.

Given the absence of time-series data, it is fair to assume that people may remain displaced for longer periods, especially if evidence confirms that their homes have been destroyed. Having such data would be valuable to assess the conditions in which IDPs are living, which in turn could be valuable to inform the costs and timeframes of reconstruction and resettlement plans. Governments could also use data to reach out to donors and financial institutions for longer-term investments.

Good examples exist throughout the region where disaster management authorities have improved their event-based monitoring of disaster impacts, allowing an understanding of how displacement evolves. The Disaster Response Operations Monitoring and Information Center of the Philippines collects information on the number of people evacuated and the number staying in shelters. This data provides humanitarian responders and development planners with vital and potentially life-saving insight into displacement flows, patterns, and IDP conditions.[167] A similar initiative was put in place in Timor-Leste following the floods associated with tropical cyclone Seroja, which provided useful insights on how long people remained displaced (Box 2).

Box 2: Reporting Following Tropical Cyclone Seroja in Timor-Leste

In late March 2021, Timor-Leste was struck by the worst flooding in 40 years, and the United Nations (UN)—in collaboration with the Secretariat of State for Civil Protection—systematically published data on the number of people temporarily sheltered.

For almost 6 months, the UN issued regular reports on the number of people in evacuation centers, providing humanitarian responders and development planners with useful information for their operations. The data showed that the number of people displaced grew from 9,700 in the immediate aftermath of the disaster to a peak of around 15,800 in early April, before falling progressively until the end of the year (Figure 25).

Even in the case of Timor-Leste, if reporting ends before the number of internally displaced people (IDPs) reaches zero, it is not known whether the remaining IDPs are still in a situation of displacement or whether they have found a durable solution. In the report issued at the end of September 2021, 701 people remained temporarily sheltered across 6 evacuation centers in Dili, which accounted for 4.4% of the peak number of people that were evacuated.[a] The people that remained sheltered were unable to return to their communities of origin, as they were deemed too disaster-prone. The absence of further reporting may have implications for the provision of protection and assistance to those who remain displaced.

a UN Timor-Leste. 2021. Timor-Leste Flood Response Situation Report No. 13.

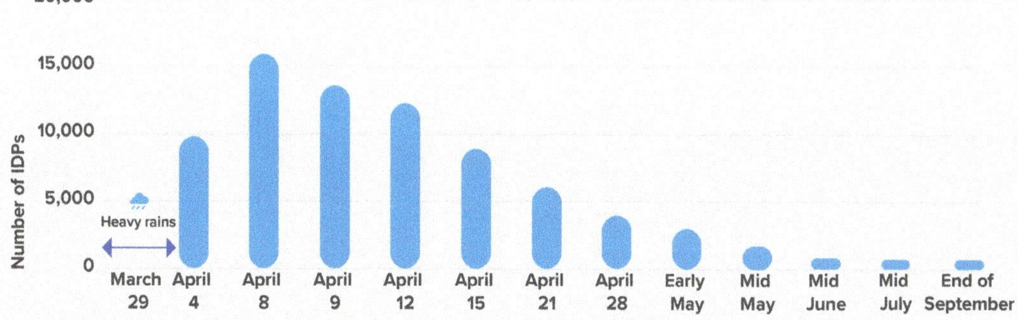

Figure 25: Number of People Displaced in Timor-Leste Following Tropical Cyclone Seroja in March 2021

Source: Internal Displacement Monitoring Centre, 2022

In both cases, a major limitation remains, which is to understand if IDPs returned, relocated elsewhere, or integrated locally into areas of destination. Beyond this lack of measurement of physical movement, it is impossible to know the conditions in which displaced people find themselves. Having such information could unveil many success stories on how disaster risk reduction and post-disaster recovery are making a positive difference in terms of durable solutions to displacement.

There are, however, some examples. The reconstruction following the Gorkha earthquake in Nepal was one of the largest reconstruction efforts worldwide and brought experiences and lessons learned that are vital to informing future post-disaster recovery, reconstruction, and durable solutions programs. A significant portion of the multi-donor trust fund established to support reconstruction focused on restoring affected houses with new homes that were built to withstand several hazards. As of 2021, the trust provided around 75% of those whose houses were destroyed by the earthquake with new and more resilient homes.[168] This example shows that having information on housing reconstruction costs and timeframes can be used to measure the achievement of durable solutions, especially returns.

Permanently relocating people out of harm's way is recognized as a long-term disaster risk reduction strategy and climate adaptation measure.[169] Whether it is planned to avert disaster impacts or post-disaster resettlement, a large body of research has shown that resettlement projects come with impoverishment risks for the communities who are moved.[170] Some of the key criteria for making these projects sustainable include assessing the complexity and high costs involved, supporting livelihoods and community cohesion, involving communities in decision-making, and ensuring they are provided with adequate and affordable housing.[171]

In June 2021, the Association of Southeast Asian Nations (ASEAN) Coordinating Centre for Humanitarian Assistance on disaster management and the Palu Municipal Government of Indonesia officially opened the ASEAN Village.[172] The village is a rehabilitation area in Tondo, Palu City consisting of 100 earthquake-resistant permanent housing units, a mosque, and a medical center. The ASEAN Village is the first regional initiative of this kind and forms one of the longer-term efforts in the region to support the recovery of the communities affected by the 2018 Central Sulawesi earthquake and tsunami. It is meant to provide an opportunity for Palu citizens to restore their livelihoods and have a safe environment to recover from the impacts of disasters, including displacement.[173]

While it may not be the preferred option for many, there are circumstances in which displaced people cannot or do not want to return or resettle elsewhere. This is the case in some communities that were displaced by riverbank erosion in Shariatpur, Bangladesh, in 2018. For many of the 43,000 IDPs, returning was not an option. To respond to this reality, the Bangladesh Red Crescent Society and the government provided cash assistance programs to both IDPs and host communities.[174] However, it remains extremely challenging to collect data on how many people are integrating locally. Initiatives supporting livelihood, education, and health programs would benefit from having this information, as it would allow responders to better identify what good practice means in the context of local integration.

Mainstreaming durable solutions to internal displacement into post-disaster recovery and reconstruction initiatives would raise the much-needed attention on those displaced by disasters and the effects of climate change. The Inter-Agency Standing Committee Framework on Durable Solutions and the recommendations from the Report of the UN Secretary-General's High-Level Panel on Internal Displacement are good bases to guide policy and action that can help bridge this gap.[175]

Displaced family in Nepal. Living conditions in emergency shelters can be particularly difficult for children, women, older people and people with disabilities. (Photo by © UNICEF/UN017119/Shrestha)

The Seasonal Nature of Disasters and Displacement

The recurrence of disasters plays a role in shaping the vulnerability of people and may also impact the response, recovery, and future risk of displacement. The seasonality of storms and monsoons in the Asia and Pacific region, for example, leaves very little time for displaced people to recover, potentially forcing them into prolonged or repeated displacement. With the prospect of climate change likely bringing possible intensification of climatic seasonality across the region—including increases in the average peak flows of monsoon-fed rivers—it is crucial to gain a better understanding of how seasonal hazards may affect displacement.[176]

Using long-term observable data to understand the frequency of weather-related hazards and the displacement they trigger provides insights into future displacement trends, as well as how they can vary over time and space. This analysis focuses on floods and storms during 1990–2021; the two hazards which trigger the most disaster displacement across the region and globally.

On average, close to 90% of the displacements triggered by floods in the Asia and Pacific region during this period took place between May and August. Much of it is the result of intense rainfall due to the Southwest monsoon in South Asia, the South Pacific cyclone season, and the East Asian rainy season triggering displacement in highly populated countries (Figure 26, blue line).

The data also sheds light on displacement associated with the different storm seasons taking place across the Asia and Pacific region throughout the year, such as the cyclone season in South Asia which tends to take place between March and May, the south Pacific cyclone season from November to April, and the Pacific typhoon season typically affecting East Asian countries between May and October (Figure 26, purple line).

Looking at subregional data, disaster displacement appears concentrated in certain months of the year, with some subregional variations (Figure 27 and Figure 28). In South Asia, for example, the data confirms that most flood-related displacement takes place between May and September. Disaggregating the data by subregion also paints an incomplete picture of the monthly frequency of displacement for the subregions having limited displacement data, such as Central and West Asia.

Using disaster displacement data to analyze the seasonal nature of disasters and displacement can be a useful tool for prevention and response. If this data is further disaggregated by location, it provides even more useful insights into where hotspots are. In Indonesia, for example, the comprehensiveness and geographical coverage of disaster displacement data provide even more detailed results, illustrating its potential to inform decision-making for risk reduction (Box 3).

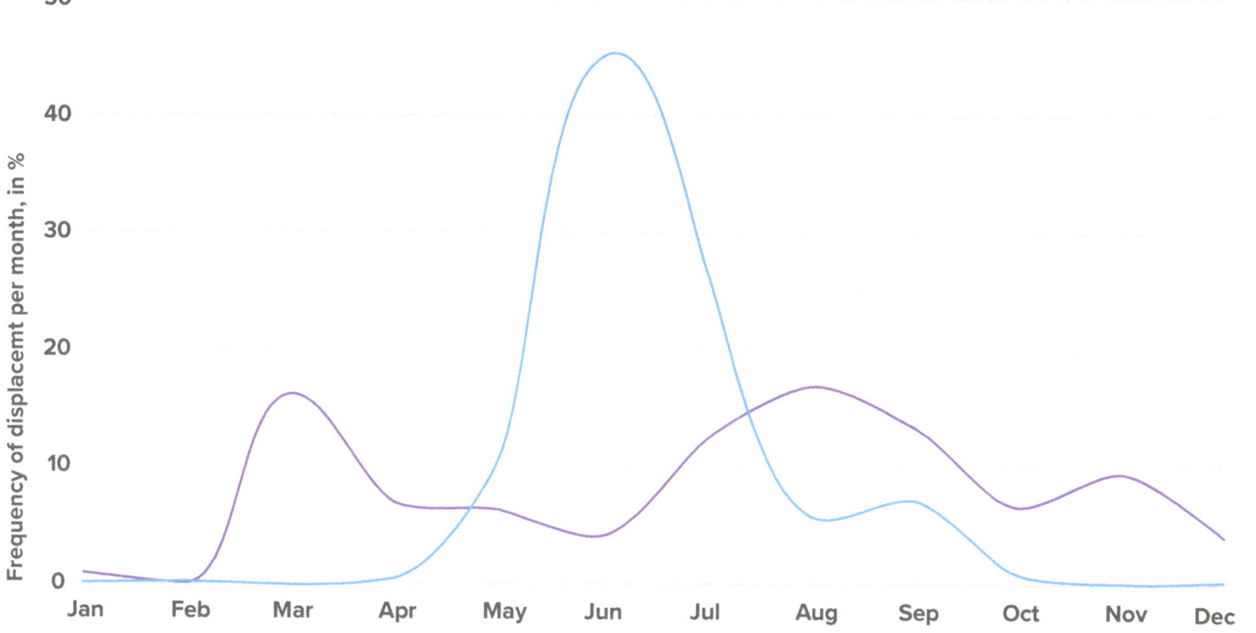

Figure 26: Frequency of Flood and Storm-related Displacement per Month in the Asia and Pacific Region (1990–2021)

Source: EM-DAT, 2022; Internal Displacement Monitoring Centre, 2022

Child displaced by Typhoon Molave. A young child plays in the damaged province of Quang Ngai, Viet Nam, after Typhoon Molave hit the area in October 2020. (Photo by © UNICEF/UN0356644/Pham/AFP-Services)

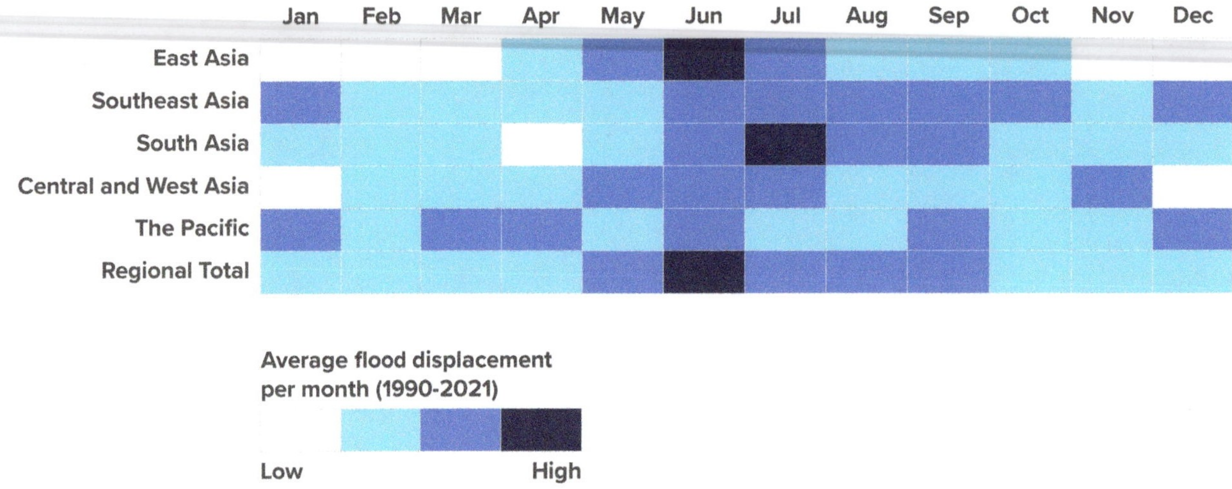

Figure 27: Frequency of Flood-related Displacement by Subregion (1990–2021)

Source: EM-DAT, 2022; Internal Displacement Monitoring Centre, 2022

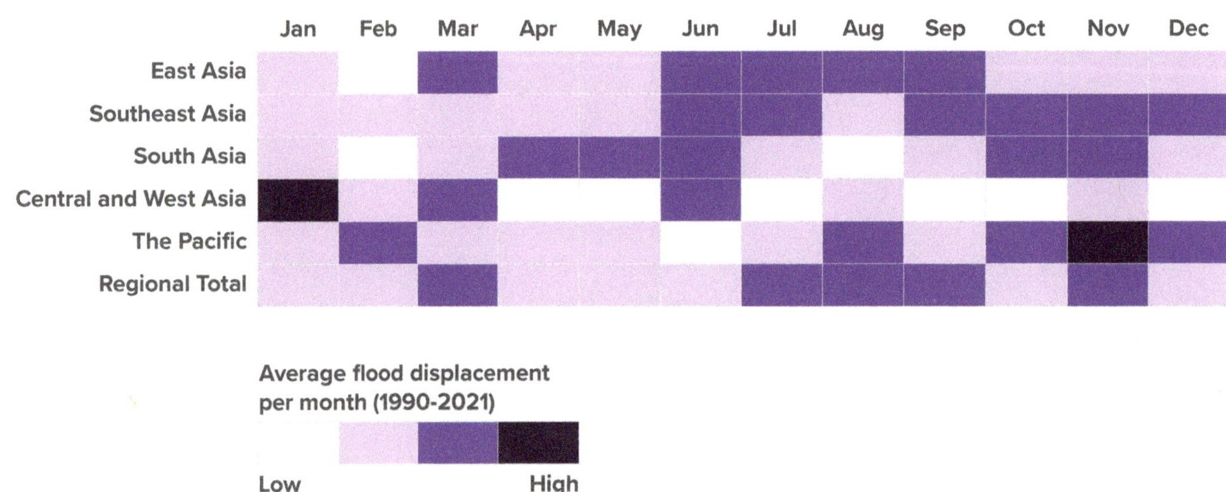

Figure 28: Frequency of Storm-related Displacement by Subregion (1990–2021)

Source: EM-DAT, 2022; Internal Displacement Monitoring Centre, 2022

Java's sinking cities
A woman stands atop sand bags keeping the sea from inundating her home in a village which was hundreds of meters away from the sea a decade ago. In the Central Java city, continued over reliance on groundwater for agriculture and industry, and climate change leading to more frequent floods are resulting in a slow motion crisis. (Photo by Ed Wray/ Getty Images)

Box 3: The Value of Data in Understanding the Seasonality of Disasters and Displacement: The Case of Indonesia

The disaster loss database of Indonesia—maintained by the National Board for Disaster Management—goes back almost 200 years with systematic reporting of disaster loss indicators such as number of evacuations, number of affected, and number of destroyed housing, among others. Having this archive is a useful starting point to better understand the impacts and dynamics of disasters.

Analyzing the number of internal displacements due to floods across the country during 1990–2021 shows an increase over 4 months: January, February, November, and December (Figure 29). These correspond to the months when rainy seasons have taken place during that same period. This is useful data that can be used for preparedness and response ahead of future rainy seasons.

This analysis can also be conducted at a subnational level, as the National Board for Disaster Management data also provides information on specific disaster events and dates, including the location where they took place. Figure 30 shows the average monthly evacuations due to flooding between 1990 and 2021, for the four provinces being the most prone to floods in the country. Displacements normally occur in Aceh at the beginning of the rainy season in November and December, while in the other three provinces they generally take place between January and February.

The Indonesian case shows how systematic collection, management, and disaggregation of data, as well as a consistent and coherent process to do so, allows for more in-depth analysis that can inform disaster risk reduction policies and actions.

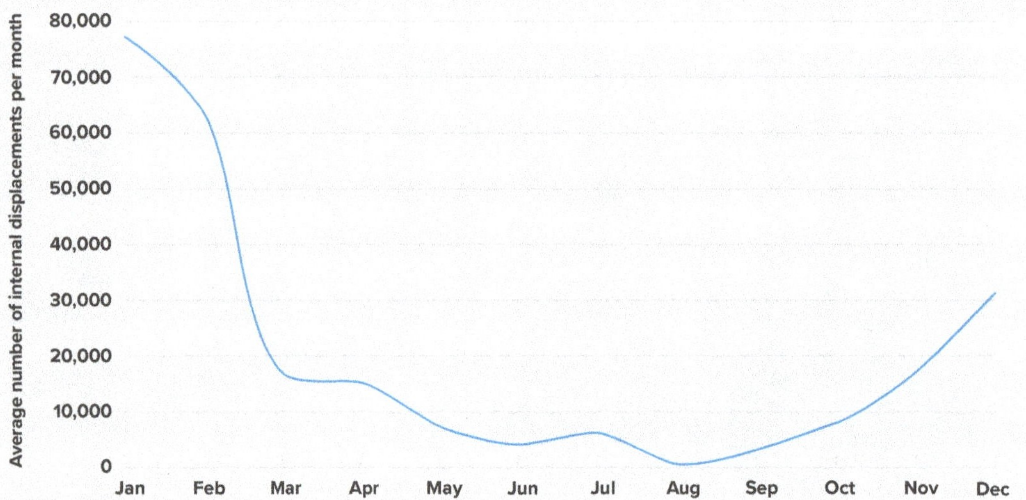

Figure 29: Frequency of Flood-related Displacements in Indonesia (1990–2021)

Source: National Board for Disaster Management of Indonesia, 2022; Internal Displacement Monitoring Centre, 2022

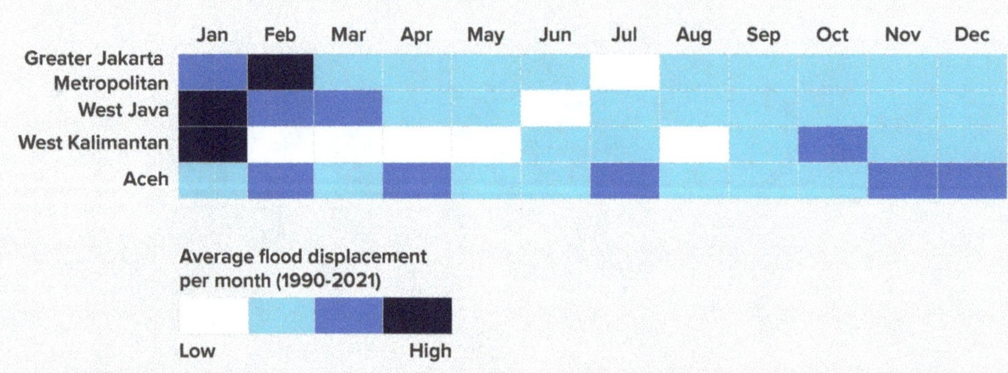

Figure 30: Frequency of Flood-related Displacements for selected provinces in Indonesia (1990–2021)

Source: National Board for Disaster Management of Indonesia, 2022; Internal Displacement Monitoring Centre, 2022

What Next? The Role of Urbanization and Climate Change in Driving Disaster Displacement

Climate change is expected to have different impacts across the Asia and Pacific region. Slow-onset hazards may lead to the gradual loss of territory and livelihoods, increased food insecurity, and water scarcity. The frequency and intensity of sudden-onset hazards may make disasters more devastating, forcing more people to move.[177]

Climate change effects are starting to become visible. Preliminary evidence shows that climate change is making certain hazards in the region more frequent and intense.[178] During the past 2 decades, 19 of the warmest years on record have occurred, and this timeframe has also overlapped with an increase in damages and losses resulting from weather-related events.[179] However, assuming that climate change is responsible for increased disaster damages, losses and displacement can be problematic for several reasons (Box 4).

There is a general agreement among scientists that—in combination with other factors—climate change is projected to increase displacement.[180] Climate anomalies such as the 2021 rainy season in the PRC, or the 2020 heatwave in Australia resulted in high numbers of people being displaced.[181]

In the world's most rapidly urbanizing region, the role of urbanization in shaping displacement risk will be critical, as it contributes significantly to increasing the exposure of people to hazards. Floods are the most common hazard affecting towns and cities around the world, which means that mitigating the risk of urban flooding would considerably reduce future disaster displacement.

In 2018, IDMC improved its global disaster displacement risk model for floods, and results show that around 80% of the people at risk of displacement associated with riverine flooding live in urban and peri-urban areas. The Asia and Pacific region has the highest risk of flood displacement, with more than 86% of those at risk living in urban and peri-urban areas.[182]

The model also allows the assessment of displacement risk at the subnational level to reveal hotspots, which—unsurprisingly—are urban areas. Dhaka, the capital of Bangladesh and home to more than nine million people, is traversed by six rivers that have been vital to trade, transport, and livelihoods for centuries. Rapid urbanization and poorly managed embankment and drainage schemes have increased the risk of flooding and waterlogging.[183]

As the city continues to expand, this risk will grow unless measures to reduce it are put in place. By revealing where flood displacement risk is concentrated in Dhaka, the results identify areas where interventions are most needed (Figure 31).

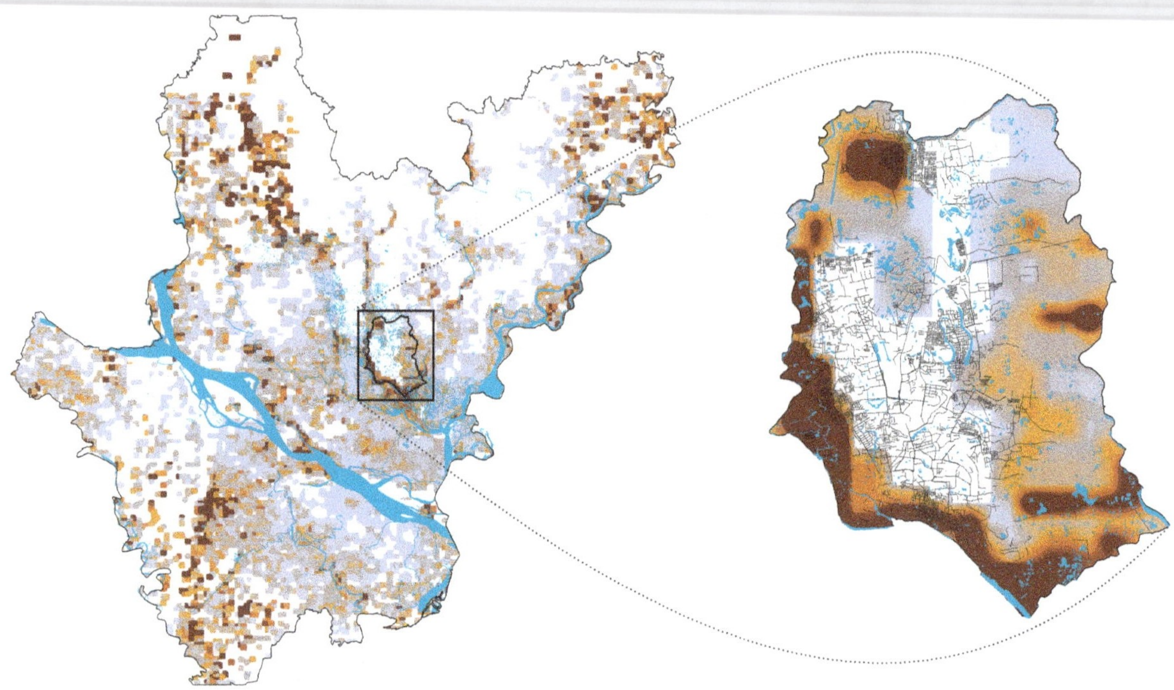

People at risk of being displaced by floods

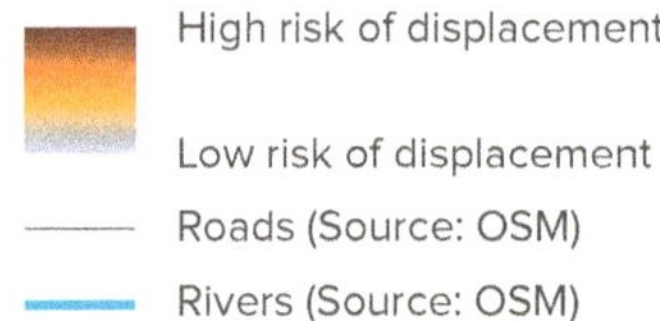

Figure 31: Flood Displacement Risk in Dhaka

Source: Internal Displacement Monitoring Centre, 2022

Heavy monsoon rains in Bangladesh. Heavy monsoon rains flooded the northern and north-eastern districts of Bangladesh in the summer of 2020, leading thousands of people into displacement. (Photo by WFP/Mehedi Rahman)

Box 4: Does Climate Change Contribute to Higher Levels of Displacement?

There is an increasing body of literature discussing the relationship between climate change, migration, and displacement.[a] One of the key aspects to consider is that the phenomenon is highly complex, making it difficult to draw causal relationships between climate change, disasters, and displacement.

One of the factors hampering comprehensive analyzes is the lack of longitudinal data. Since little more than a decade ago countries in the region started to enhance their disaster monitoring and reporting capacities, providing a more solid evidence base on disaster impacts, including displacement. The increasing trends in disaster damages, losses, and displacement observed in the last years can therefore be attributed to efforts by governments to implement and maintain disaster loss databases. Assuming that such an increase in data translates into increased displacement could be problematic, as it may be the case that a high number of displacements happened in the past, but no records are available. As a result, nuances are needed when it comes to analyzing trends.

In addition, as the climate varies naturally from year to year, climatologists use standard 30-year averages of temperatures, precipitation, humidity, and wind speed that are known as "climate normals" to summarize average climatic conditions.[b] However, disaster displacement data have only been available in Asia and the Pacific since about 2008, making it impossible to establish a direct correlation with longer-term climate trends.

Looking ahead, a multitude of demographic, historical, political, social, and economic factors will determine whether people can withstand the impacts of future weather-related hazards driven by climate variability and change. However, it should also be looked at with other risk drivers including poverty and vulnerability, unsustainable urbanization, land degradation and erosion, to name only a few. Consequently, a deeper understanding of the multi-layered and interdependent nature of these drivers, and how climate change shapes displacement patterns, is therefore needed.

Sources:

a See IDMC GRID 2021. Internal Displacement in a Changing Climate; V. Clement et al. 2021. Groundswell Part 2: Acting on Internal Climate Migration. World Bank: Washington, D.C.; and IPCC. 2022. Climate Change 2022: Impacts, Adaptation and Vulnerability. Contribution of Working Group II Contribution to the IPCC Sixth Assessment Report, which include a large number of reference documents and analysis.

b World Meteorological Organization (WMO). 2015. New Two-Tier approach on "climate normals".

Other assessments have shown how the urban expansion is overlapping with hazard intensity, increasing the risk of displacement. In the Vanuatu capital of Port Vila, rapid urbanization has resulted in high population density in exposed and vulnerable areas of the city. Peri-urban areas are growing at twice the rate of Port Vila, and so are nearby villages outside the city limits. Informal housing and deficits in services and infrastructure, combined with population density, are increasing the exposure of people to a wide range of hazards, which is, in turn, increasing their overall disaster displacement risk.[184]

Using displacement risk metrics can allow decision-makers to inform planning and investments in disaster risk reduction at the local, national, and global levels. This will help to prevent displacement and reduce its impacts. To further refine the analysis, risk models could take into consideration population growth and climate change scenarios.

Research from ETH Zurich provides an approximation of the potential impacts that climate change may have in increasing the risk of displacement associated with floods in Asia and the Pacific. The model estimates that the flood displacement risk as of 2022 has already doubled compared with the baseline (Figure 32). By the end of the century, the risk is expected to remain relatively similar to that of today. This projection is under the most optimistic scenario where climate change would be strongly mitigated (RCP2.6) and the region shifts towards sustainable social and economic development (SSP1). Under the worst-case scenario, with weak mitigation of climate change (RCP6.0) and unsustainable development (SSP4), flood displacement risk is expected to increase more than twice by the end of the century.

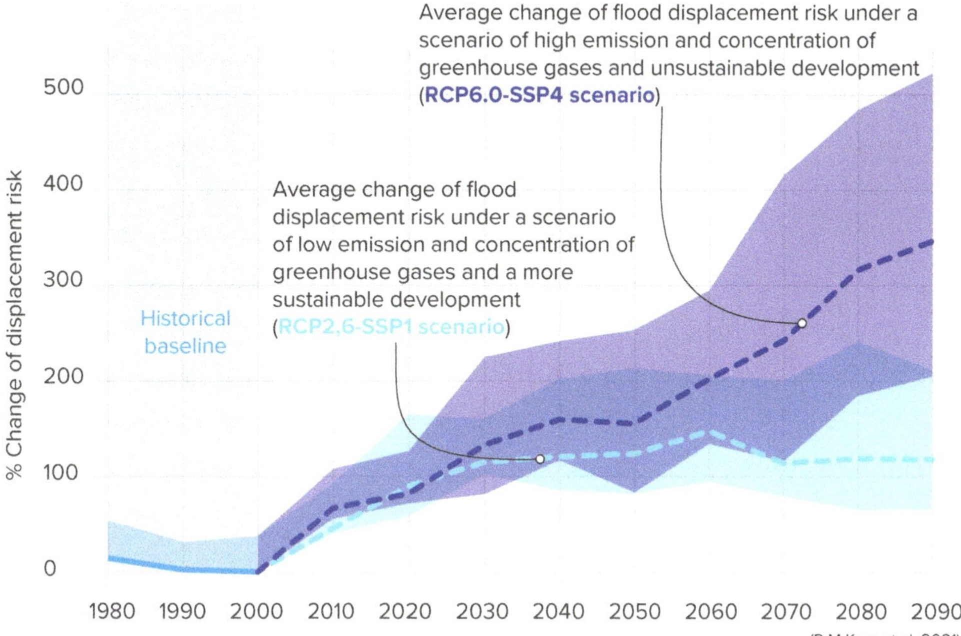

What is this graph showing?

This graph shows changes in flood displacement risk compared to historical baseline data. Shaded areas show the different scenarios of flood displacement risk in response to variations in greenhouse gas concentrations, global hydrological systems and social and economic development pathways. Dashed lines show the average values.

Key definitions:

Historical Baseline: The models are tested by simulating the historical baseline calculated with flood hazard frequency and intensity, from 1976 to 2005, and population data of 2000.

Representative Concentration Pathways (RCP): Describe 21st century pathways in terms of greenhouse gas emissions and atmospheric concentrations, other air pollutant emissions and land use change, as per the IPCC.

Shared Socio-economic Pathways (SSP): Describe scenarios of future socioeconomic and demographic conditions.

RCP6.0-SSP4 scenario: Means a high greenhouse gas emissions rate with a highly unequal development path.

RCP2.6-SSP1 scenario: Means stronger greenhouse gas mitigation efforts where the world shifts towards a more sustainable development path. This scenario aims to keep global warming below 2°C above pre-industrial temperatures.

Figure 32: Changes in Flood Displacement Risk in Asia and the Pacific Considering Different Climate and Development Scenarios

Source: ETH Zurich, 2022; Internal Displacement Monitoring Centre, 2022

Other studies suggest that extreme weather events could occur that lie outside all model predictions, with impacts beyond what has been seen or expected.[185] It is important to note that not only do all these models have high levels of uncertainty but most are likely to produce underestimates.

Given that the trajectory of greenhouse gas emissions is close to the Intergovernmental Panel on Climate Change worst-case scenario, a vast amount of adaptation will be required to offset the impacts of climate change and projected population growth in flood-prone areas of the Asia and Pacific region.[186]

Part 4

Addressing Disaster Displacement: Progress in Policy and the Way Forward

Investing in development to prevent displacement. Investments in local development projects and sustainable livelihood opportunities for at-risk communities, such as coastal communities and islanders, can reduce the scale of future displacement. (Photo by the Asian Development Bank)

The Sendai Framework: 7 Years On

Adopted at the Third UN World Conference on Disaster Risk Reduction in 2015, the Sendai Framework for Disaster Risk Reduction set the global agenda for addressing both natural and human-made hazards to reduce the impact of disasters on lives, livelihoods, and economies over the following 15 years. It identifies four priorities that are key to reducing and preventing disaster risk: (i) understanding disaster risk; (ii) strengthening disaster risk governance to manage disaster risk; (iii) investing in disaster reduction for resilience and; (iv) enhancing disaster preparedness for effective response, and to "Build Back Better" in recovery, rehabilitation, and reconstruction.[187]

To measure progress in achieving the objectives of the framework, seven global targets were agreed upon:

(A) Substantially reduce global disaster mortality by 2030, aiming to lower the average per 100,000 global mortality rate in the decade 2020–2030 compared to the period 2005–2015;

(B) Substantially reduce the number of affected people globally by 2030, aiming to lower the average global figure per 100,000 in the decade 2020–2030 compared to the period 2005–2015;

(C) Reduce direct disaster economic loss in relation to global gross domestic product (GDP) by 2030;

(D) Substantially reduce disaster damage to critical infrastructure and disruption of basic services, among them health and educational facilities, including through developing their resilience by 2030;

(E) Substantially increase the number of countries with national and local disaster risk reduction strategies by 2020;

(F) Substantially enhance international cooperation with developing countries through adequate and sustainable support to complement their national actions for implementation of the present framework by 2030;

(G) Substantially increase the availability of and access to multi-hazard early warning systems and disaster risk information and assessments to people by 2030.[188]

As the midway point of the Sendai Framework implementation period approaches, countries in the Asia and Pacific region continue to face notable challenges in achieving the targets. This chapter analyzes the Sendai Framework concerning disaster displacement and assesses progress made in this regard by countries in the Asia and Pacific region.

Monitoring Progress and Data Gaps

The Sendai Framework Monitor includes no specific indicator on the number of people displaced, evacuated, or relocated, but the indicators that measure people affected by disasters under target B do include the number of houses damaged or destroyed, which can be a useful proxy for measuring the number of people affected by disaster displacement.[189] Recent recommendations from the United Nations Office for Disaster Risk Reduction (UNDRR) for monitoring progress on implementation of the Sendai Framework highlight the importance of including indicators on displacement to complement existing indicators and support people-centered approaches to achieving the seven targets.[190] Specifically, they recommend data be collected on four key indicators:

(i) The number of people pre-emptively evacuated;
(ii) The number of people displaced during and after disasters;
(iii) The number of houses destroyed;
(iv) The duration of displacement.

The International Organization for Migration and IDMC are working together in partnership with key governmental and non-governmental counterparts to develop a tested set of standard displacement-related metrics and indicators that will strengthen the ability of DRR actors to integrate displacement in their work (Box 5).[191]

Box 5: Developing Indicators for Displacement Risk Reduction

The relevance of displacement—and the need for its integration into disaster risk reduction—is well reflected in the Sendai Framework for Disaster Risk Reduction. Despite concrete mentions—and the growing centrality displacement has assumed in disaster risk reduction conversations and processes in the years since the adoption of the framework—displacement is still missing from global monitoring efforts on disaster risk reduction (DRR). There are no standardized measurements and indicators to capture the relevance of displacement implications for DRR planning and implementation as of 2022.

A better understanding of displacement could provide the DRR community with a strong people-centered marker of disaster risk and impacts, allowing it to better identify where—and what—efforts are needed to reduce the vulnerability that is associated with (or revealed by) displacement. It would also allow leverage of the life-saving, protective nature of moving in the face of a hazard while minimizing related individual risks and collective costs. The need for safe, unhindered mobility in the context of disasters has never been more apparent than as a consequence of the coronavirus disease (COVID-19) pandemic, as related mobility restrictions have resulted in immobility, vulnerability, and additional suffering for all those affected.

Source: IOM. 2022. Developing indicators on displacement and disaster risk reduction.

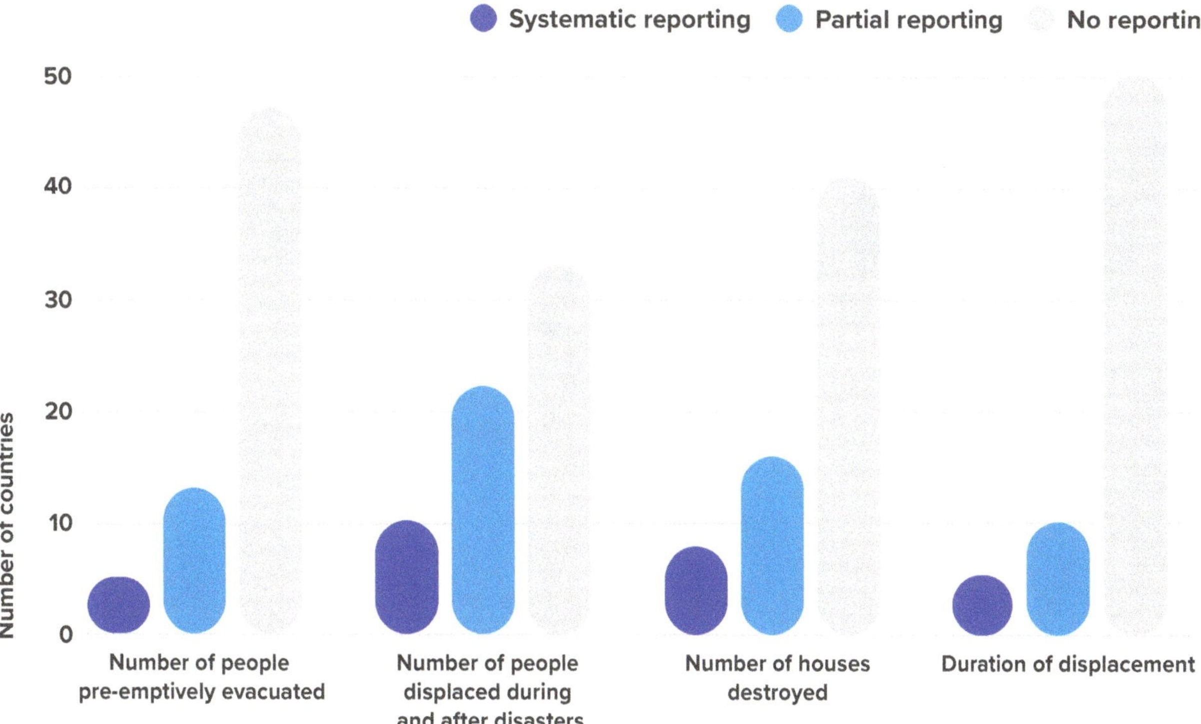

Figure 33: United Nations Office for Disaster Risk Reduction-recommended Indicators Complementing the Sendai Framework for 65 countries in the Asia and Pacific Region

Source: United Nations Office for Disaster Risk Reduction, Sendai Monitor

An assessment of 65 countries in the Asia and Pacific region found that as of 2021 only four countries reported on all four indicators mentioned above, with almost half not reporting on any of the indicators. The duration of displacement was the most significant gap, with only five countries systematically reporting on this, and a further 10 providing partial data.[192] There is also a lack of information on pre-emptive evacuations, with 47 countries not reporting any data on this (Figure 33).

While these indicators are a useful addition to the Sendai Framework Monitor, they are not enough to effectively understand and address disaster displacement. In an attempt to bridge the gap in monitoring progress on internal displacement more broadly, in 2020 IDMC developed a composite measure, the Internal Displacement Index (IDI). The IDI brings together indicators of national policies and capacities to address internal displacement, data on IDPs, contextual drivers, and impacts of displacement.[193]

An assessment of the IDI indicators on disaster displacement data for 65 countries in the Asia and Pacific region found a significant gap in both availability and quality. In almost two-thirds of countries assessed, governments do not publish or endorse data on internal displacement associated with disasters (Figure 34).

Of the data that does exist, only three countries collect data that is partially disaggregated by sex and age.[194] Such information is critical for enabling an evidence-based approach to designing, implementing, and assessing policies on disaster displacement, and should be a minimum requirement for data collection systems (Box 6).

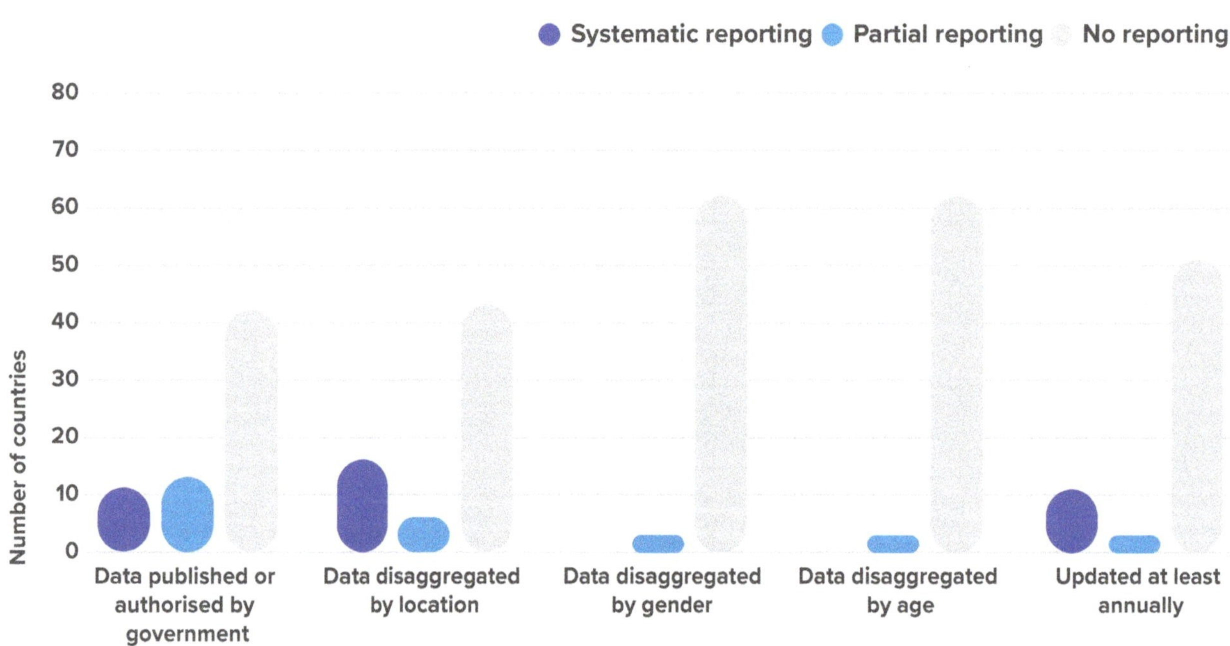

Figure 34: Internal Displacement Index Indicators on Disaster Displacement Data for 65 Countries in the Asia and Pacific Region

Source: Internal Displacement Monitoring Centre, 2022

Box 6: Where does the Internal Displacement Monitoring Centre's disaster displacement data come from?

The Internal Displacement Monitoring Centre (IDMC) collects data from a wide range of sources, including United Nations agencies, governments, the Red Cross and Red Crescent movement, international and local nongovernmental organizations, and media sources. As these organizations are engaged in a broad spectrum of humanitarian and development work, the types of movement and metrics they report differ widely.

IDMC distinguishes between the source, where the information comes from, and where it is published. In Asia and the Pacific, over 60% of the data that IDMC uses to compile its estimates for disaster displacements are published by national and regional disaster management authorities. The second type of publisher is the media, which published 14% of disaster displacement figures in the region (Figure 35). This shows a positive sign, which is that governments are doing significant efforts in making their data available, by publishing reports that allow to assess the scope and scale of disaster displacement and inform policy making.

Breaking down the sources of disaster displacement by subregion unveils significant differences in data collection (Figure 36). While in Southeast Asia, South Asia, and East Asia most disaster displacement data comes from national and regional disaster agencies, in Central and West Asia and the Pacific displacement data comes from numerous sources, including the UN, local and national governments, and the media. Subregional analyzes of data sources, however, may hide important differences among countries. This is for instance the case in Central and West Asia, where 95% of the Afghanistan data comes from the UN, while the share is marginal in other countries like Pakistan.

Moving forward, government-led efforts to collect and publish data should be continued, and partnerships to make data interoperable should be leveraged, to have the harmonized metrics, standards, and reporting periods that enable regional cooperation for displacement risk reduction.

Figure 35: Sources and Publishers of Disaster Displacement Data in the Asia and Pacific Region

Source: Internal Displacement Monitoring Centre, 2022

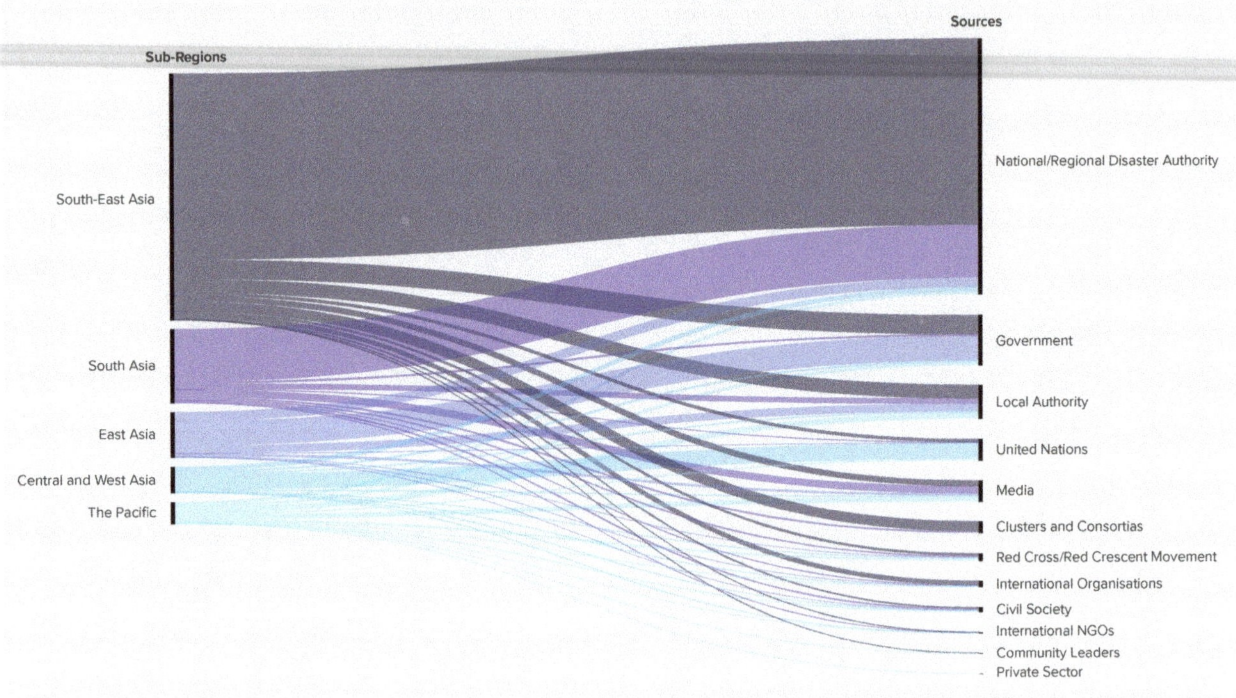

Figure 36: Sources of Disaster Displacement Data in Asia and Pacific, by Subregion

Source: Internal Displacement Monitoring Centre, 2022

National capacity to monitor disaster displacement can be increased through cooperation and sharing of knowledge and experience between governments in the region. The Regional Consultative Committee on Disaster Displacement, for instance, promotes the exchange of expertise amongst peers and offers capacity building to policymakers across the region.[195] Governments can also seek the support of international organizations to complement their efforts to monitor and address disaster displacement.

Following tropical cyclone Harold, the National Disaster Management Office of Vanuatu partnered with the International Organization for Migration (IOM) to conduct an assessment of the displaced population in both evacuation centers and host families.[196] The detailed analysis captured a comprehensive breakdown by age group, sex, disability status, and location, while also identifying key characteristics of vulnerability such as the number of pregnant and lactating individuals, unaccompanied minors, and orphans. The assessment also addressed the duration of displacement, the percentage of houses damaged or destroyed, the intentions of displaced populations, and barriers to returning.[197]

This level of detailed analysis of the situation can better inform both the immediate response and medium- to long-term planning to help affected people to access durable solutions. It can also provide the basis for applying an intersectional approach to displacement data. This requires understanding the inequalities that exist in a given context, the systems and power structures that include or exclude a person or group, and how these can influence how the impacts of displacement are experienced.[198]

For more evidence-informed policymaking to reduce disaster and displacement risk, governments in the region need to collect more and better-quality data that can help them to understand the vulnerabilities and impacts. Combining solid data and evidence with comprehensive policies and the institutional arrangements necessary for implementing them provides the strongest foundation for overcoming the challenge of disaster displacement in an increasingly hazard-prone region.

In the aftermath of Tropical Cyclone Harold. Tropical Cyclone Harold devastated Vanuatu's Pentecost in April 2020, displacing thousands of people. (Photo by UNICEF/UNI323273/Shing)

Box 7: Displaced People Require Interventions to be Tailored to their Location, Age, Gender, Ethnicity, Socioeconomic Background, and Other Characteristics

Collecting age, sex, and disability-disaggregated data on internally displaced people (IDPs) is a first step to ensuring tailored responses and better inclusion, but such data is hard to come by. In many countries in the Asia and Pacific region, information on the number of IDPs is derived from housing destruction information: the average number of people per household can be applied to the number of houses destroyed to estimate the total number of IDPs. This is a useful method to quickly get a sense of the scale of the issue, but it does not show exactly how many men, women, children, or older people are affected.

In the absence of more precise information on the age and sex of displaced people, national demographic data can be applied to the total number of IDPs to estimate how many of them are children, young people, older people, and so on. Figure 37 presents these estimates for people displaced by disasters at the end of 2021 in the Asia and Pacific region.

A comparison between the age of IDPs in IDMC surveys with the age of IDPs derived from national data does not show large differences, therefore confirming that national data can be useful to estimate age groups amongst IDPs (Figure 38).

Relying solely on national demographic data to estimate the number of IDPs of different sex, age groups, and abilities does not allow the identification of overlapping vulnerabilities, such as instances when people from particular ethnic groups may be at higher risk of being displaced and therefore overrepresented in displaced populations; or people identifying as non-binary genders facing increased threats in displacement, although they are invisible in data.

Being "displaced" comes with frequent challenges, but these challenges are not systematic, and their severity varies greatly depending on the pre-existing conditions and characteristics of people, in addition to being displaced. This makes intersectional approaches to data and analyzes on internal displacement essential to effective preventative measures, responses, and solutions.

Figure 37: Total Number of People Internally Displaced by Disasters in Asia and the Pacific at the End of 2021 by Age Group

Source: Internal Displacement Monitoring Centre, with data from the 2019 Revision of World Population Prospects produced by the Population Division of the Department of Economic and Social Affairs of the United Nations Secretariat

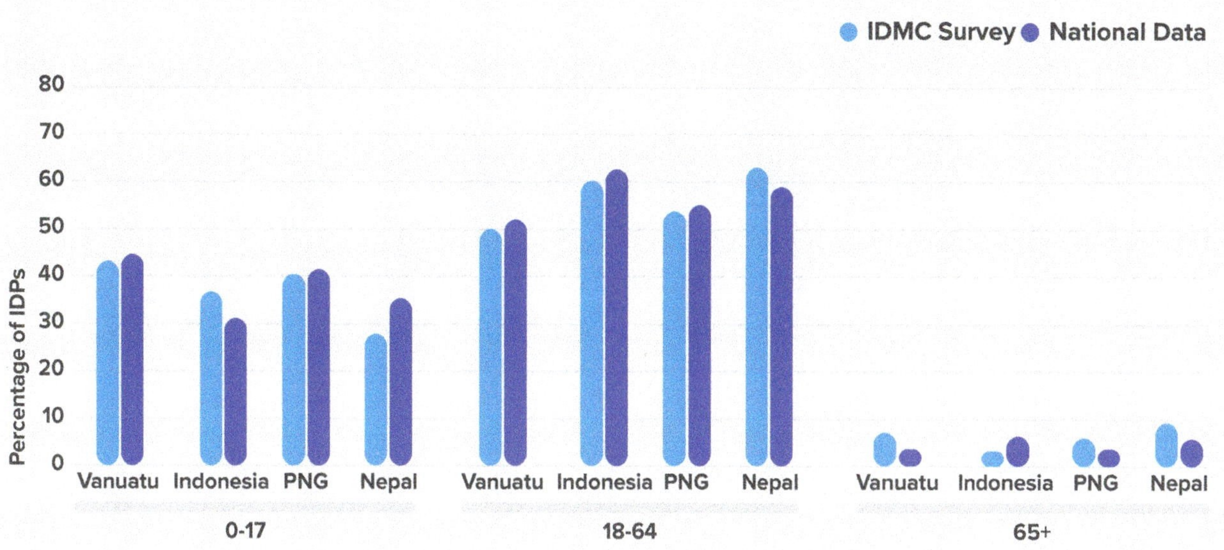

Figure 38: Comparison Between the Age of Internally Displaced People in Surveys Conducted by the Internal Displacement Monitoring Centre in 2021–2022 and National Age Distribution from the UN Population Database (World Population Prospect)

Source: Internal Displacement Monitoring Centre, with data from the 2019 Revision of World Population Prospects produced by the Population Division of the Department of Economic and Social Affairs of the United Nations Secretariat

Comprehensive Policies for Addressing Disaster Displacement

Key to achieving national progress is the adoption and implementation of policies and strategies on disaster risk reduction that align with the Sendai Framework, monitored through target E. Approaching the midway point of the Sendai Framework implementation period, there is clear evidence of countries in the region adopting new or revised policies and strategies that incorporate the globally agreed goals and priorities. Given that displacement is one of the most frequent impacts of disasters, it is a critical component of a comprehensive national framework on disaster risk reduction and management.[199]

The IDI monitors the progress of countries on the inclusion of internal displacement in national policies, including measures for prevention of further displacement, mitigation of the impacts of displacement on other groups, and efforts to achieve durable solutions. Including disaster displacement in national frameworks is not only a sign that a country recognizes an issue and is willing to address it, but also indicates an ability to do so. Without plans to prevent, prepare for, and respond to disaster displacement, ad hoc initiatives to mitigate its negative consequences are likely to be insufficient and unsustainable. Comprehensive policies should include preventive measures and provisions to end displacement and limit its negative consequences on IDPs and other affected people.

An assessment of the legal and policy frameworks of 23 countries found that the majority (87%) recognize internal displacement caused by disasters (Figure 39). Approximately two-thirds include measures to prevent future displacement and to address durable solutions. Less than half include measures to mitigate the impact of displacement on other groups, such as host communities. Figure 39 shows the average IDI policy indicator value for each country assessed, where one is the best possible score.[200]

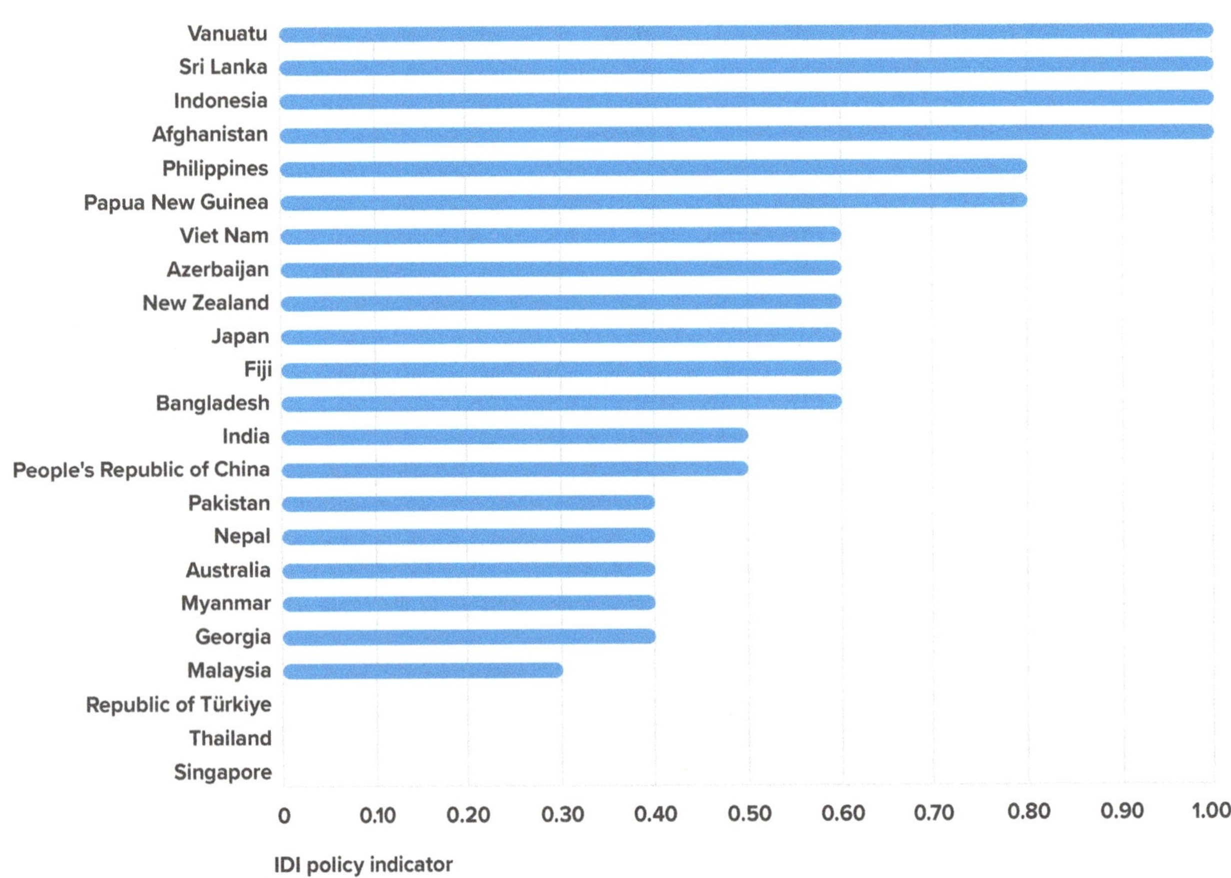

Figure 39: Internal Displacement Index Indicator on Policy for 23 Countries Assessed

Source: Internal Displacement Monitoring Centre, 2022

Some promising examples of comprehensive policies and strategies that address disaster displacement are emerging in the region. These include the latest update to the Philippines National Disaster Risk Management Plan for 2020–2030, which specifically sets out to incorporate the Sendai Framework commitments and priorities, as well as other global, regional, and national agendas.[201] The revised plan includes measures to prevent and respond to disaster displacement and achieve durable solutions for IDPs. It is complemented by the National Climate Change Action Plan for 2011–2028, which also recognizes displacement as a result of climate change and increased exposure to disasters, as well as the potential for conflict over natural resources.[202] It includes measures to prevent displacement, achieve durable solutions for displaced people and populations resettled as a result of climate change adaptation, and mitigate the negative consequences on other affected groups.

The Bangladesh 2016–2020 National Plan for Disaster Management (NPDM) was explicitly aligned with the Sendai Framework.[203] Priority 4 of the plan called for an inclusive recovery and rehabilitation strategy for disaster-affected and displaced households to address their short- and long-term recovery needs.[204] It required the creation of a national database on displacement, including sex, age, and disability disaggregated data. The updated NPDM for 2021–2025 maintains this alignment and the inclusion of disaster displacement while placing greater emphasis on the link between climate change and rapid urbanization.[205]

This is supported by the National Strategy on the Management of Disaster and Climate-Induced Internal Displacement (2015), which seeks to prevent and respond to displacement and support the achievement of durable solutions through housing assistance, livelihood opportunities, and improved community infrastructure.[206] It emphasizes the importance of addressing the impact of displacement and relocation on host communities, providing them with social security assistance, and engaging them in local integration interventions.[207]

Although not all countries have developed standalone policies on internal displacement, many have included provisions on internal displacement in their disaster management plans and disaster risk reduction (DRR) frameworks. The National Disaster Management Plan of India, updated in 2019, recognizes disaster displacement and the need to prevent subsequent displacement when responding to disasters.[208] It includes measures for the socioeconomic rehabilitation of affected communities and recognizes the impacts of displacement on people with disabilities, children, women, and older people.

The region also leads the way in its inclusion of internal displacement in climate change policies and in harnessing human mobility as an adaptation strategy. The 2012 National Climate Change Policy of Pakistan acknowledges displacement as a result of the effects of climate change and includes prevention measures.[209]

The National Climate Change Policy 2018–2030 and the National Adaptation Plan of Fiji both recognize the impacts of climate change on displacement and call for targeted action to protect communities most at risk.[210] The Fiji National Planned Relocation Guidelines establish processes for addressing the risk of climate and disaster-driven displacement.[211]

Many countries in the region have highlighted their commitment to fulfilling the call of the Sendai Framework to incorporate gender, age, disability, and cultural perspective into policies and practices. DRR frameworks and strategies in countries such as Fiji, New Zealand, and Papua New Guinea highlight the need to pay special attention to people disproportionately affected by disasters, including people with disabilities, women, children, and youth, and to include them in the design of policies and plans to build resilience and manage risks before, during and after disasters.[212]

Translating Words into Action

Going beyond the adoption of comprehensive policies, these must be translated into effective action through the necessary institutional arrangements and funding mechanisms. Some promising examples that are emerging in the region to address displacement and reduce further risk include Viet Nam, which has developed policies to integrate evacuation and relocation into its DRR and climate change adaptation strategy. It has widely implemented planned relocations to reduce the risk of flooding since the early 1990s.[213] In doing so, it has demonstrated how adopting an inclusive and participatory approach to resettlement can reduce its disruption to lives and generate positive long-term results.[214]

The Vanuatu 2018 national policy on climate change and disaster-induced displacement stands as one of the most detailed policies in the region.[215] It provides a common framework to assist all people affected by displacement and sets out strategic priority areas for interventions aimed at addressing displacement and facilitating the successful return of IDPs, their local integration, or their planned relocation.[216] In promoting an evidence-based approach to displacement, it calls for a displacement tracking mechanism to collect disaggregated data on people affected by displacement, including host communities.[217]

Several countries have also developed financing instruments to ensure sufficient resources are allocated to implement policy goals and address displacement risks and impacts. The National Disaster Risk Reduction and Management Fund of the Philippines supports a range of activities including aid and relief services, improving the construction of evacuation centers, and recovery and rehabilitation.[218] Local disaster risk reduction and management funds in the Philippines also encourage local government investment in disaster risk reduction.[219]

Such examples are encouraging, and more needs to be done in terms of implementation and follow-up. For instance, a review of gender-responsive and disability-inclusive progress toward Sendai Framework targets in 26 countries in the Asia and Pacific region found that implementation was limited and that coordination between stakeholders on inclusive DRR is still lacking.[220] Leveraging indigenous knowledge and the participation of communities affected by disasters and displacement is key to ensuring the relevance, efficiency, and sustainability of national and local efforts to reduce disaster risk and adapt to climate change (Box 8).

Box 8: The Participation of Indigenous People in Preventing and Responding to Disaster Displacement in Asia and the Pacific

Participation of indigenous communities in designing and implementing internal displacement policies is essential. When it comes to climate change, for instance, there is growing awareness that they are not only among the first victims of displacement but that they are also agents of environmental conservation, adaptation, and mitigation.[a] Their understanding of natural cycles, the environment, livelihoods, and food systems, as well as their adaptation to changing environmental patterns, contributes to the protection of biodiversity and the reduction of displacement risk. Their ancestral knowledge passed down intergenerationally can play an important role in prevention, forecasting, and response efforts.[b]

Ancestral practices have helped these communities prepare for disasters and prevent displacement for thousands of years. After the 2004 Indian Ocean tsunami, a plethora of research was conducted on indigenous disaster risk reduction. Findings showed that the Moken communities of Surin island in Thailand, the Simeulueans in Indonesia, and many island populations of Andaman and Nicobar islands successfully predicted the tsunami and employed their traditional strategies to effectively cope with its impacts.[c]

In the Gandak river basin of India, community members interpret observations of ant activity, fish behavior, river levels, water color, rainfall, wind direction, and the orientation of rain-related star constellations to forecast floods.[d] Such examples highlight that indigenous knowledge and ancestral practices can help communities adapt to the impacts of climate change and reduce their risk of displacement.

Sources:

a UN Human Rights Council. 2017. Report of the Special Rapporteur on the rights of indigenous peoples. Impacts of climate change and climate finance, A/ HRC/36/46; L. Etchart. 2017. The role of indigenous peoples in combating climate change. Palgrave Commun. 3. Art. 17085. 22 August.

b UN Permanent Forum on Indigenous Issues 2013. Study on Engaging Indigenous Peoples More Inclusively in the Disaster Risk Reduction Process.

c N. Arunotai. 2008. Saved by an old legend and a keen observation: the case of Moken sea nomads in Thailand; S. Lambert and J. Scott. 2019. International disaster risk reduction strategies and Indigenous Peoples.

d M. A. Chen. 1991. Coping with seasonality and drought. Delhi: SAGE.

The Way Forward

Reviewing gaps in government efforts to monitor and address internal displacement helps to identify a few immediate action points to be considered across Asia and the Pacific:

- Enhance data collection and analysis on disaster displacement to systematically record the scale and severity of the phenomenon, as well as its impacts on people and economies;
- Develop national policy frameworks on disaster displacement to ensure immediate, comprehensive, and inclusive support to IDPs;
- Invest in the planning and financing of durable solutions to disaster displacement, including options for return to areas of origin, or integration in host communities or other areas;
- Assess the risk of future disaster displacement and its potential consequences on people and economies to develop more effective, comprehensive, and inclusive prevention plans and allocate adequate resources in vulnerable areas;
- Strengthen regional collaboration on disaster displacement and foster the sharing of knowledge, experience, and expertise across Asia and the Pacific.

There are signs of renewed regional commitment and multi-stakeholder collaboration that could accelerate action to prevent and respond to disaster displacement more effectively. The Asian Disaster Preparedness Center and the United Nations Office for Disaster Risk Reduction signed a Statement of Cooperation in August 2021 to strengthen the implementation of the Sendai Framework, promote climate and disaster resilience, and improve risk governance across Asia and the Pacific.[221] Fostering greater accountability and monitoring and evaluating progress on internal displacement in Asia and the Pacific is key to addressing what should be considered one of the most significant challenges of the region.

Although the COVID-19 pandemic is likely to put a strain on resources in years to come, this should not divert attention away from the urgent need for actors in the region to fulfill their commitments, nor should it prevent them from doing so. Maximizing funds and working collaboratively to deliver on policy goals and ensure investments are targeted, strategic, and effective will be more necessary than ever before.

The Asia Regional Plan for implementation of the Sendai Framework, developed by the International Strategy for Disaster Reduction Asia Partnership and a regional advisory working group, sets out clear goals and milestones in 2-year intervals, creating a regional roadmap for achieving the seven targets.[222] The latest action plan (2021–2024) notes that climate- and disaster-related displacement is increasing and calls for the inclusion of displacement prevention as a key element of disaster risk reduction strategies, emphasizing a rights-based and inclusive approach.[223]

The mid-term review of the Sendai Framework implementation is underway as of 2022, with results to be presented to the UN General Assembly in 2023. This provides an opportunity to take stock of the progress, challenges, and implementation gaps, and potentially put disaster displacement back on the agenda.

Conclusion

Disaster displacement is a significant challenge for Asia and the Pacific. This report shows that despite some variations in the numbers from year to year, the overall scale of displacement from floods, cyclones, tsunamis, droughts, and earthquakes has remained unchanged for more than a decade. As more people settle in hazard-prone areas, thereby increasing their exposure to disaster displacement risk, efforts to protect them and reduce their vulnerability will not be sufficient. In addition, the impacts of climate change will influence future weather patterns and extremes, acting as additional stressors on environmental and socio-economic systems.

The region, however, also has unique opportunities to meet these challenges. The urban nature of displacement highlights the key role that urban planning and municipal administrations and services can play in preventive action and improved response. Rather than relying on humanitarian response delivered by an already over-stretched international system and limited national capacities, pre-emptive action through community resilience-building, investing in disaster risk reduction, early warning systems, and climate action will be the only viable strategies.

The evidence presented in this report further shows that frameworks for action exist at national, regional, and global levels. The Sendai Framework for Disaster Risk Reduction and related guidance provide countries with the tools to manage disaster risk and therefore displacement. In the context of climate change negotiations, disaster displacement is starting to be recognized as an issue of not just human security and human rights, but of global justice and common concern.

What is needed now is a more explicit inclusion of displacement as a key feature of disaster risk in national planning and investments. The direct and indirect cost of displacement from disasters must be factored into preparedness and contingency planning and long-term development planning processes. This will be difficult to achieve without reliable data on the numbers of people displaced and at risk of displacement, and the potential impacts and associated costs.

Countries and their partners will need to identify the metrics and indicators to measure and monitor displacement and displacement risk, use the data for planning and response, and track progress systematically. In particular, the cyclical nature of disasters in the region means that analysis of the seasonality of disaster displacement must be better used to inform policies and operations. For this, more and better data are required to analyze where people may be displaced and when, and the factors that prolong their displacement. Understanding the role that climate change impacts will have on these patterns in the future will also be key.

Countries are increasingly recognizing the need for trusted and actionable evidence on displacement, and a growing number of disaster-related policies and operational efforts acknowledge the need for data. However, displacement-related metrics are not included in national indicators that are used to monitor progress against disaster risk reduction targets. Moreover, no country assesses the cost of displacement consistently and systematically. New initiatives at the country and international level presented in this report are emerging and are starting to fill this gap, presenting a step in the right direction.

These good practices can and need to be built on. Political, technical, and financial support will be required to support these efforts, both from the countries of the region and their regional and global partners. Asia and the Pacific accounts for the vast majority of disaster displacements globally; therefore, if disaster displacement across the world needs to be addressed, it needs to start here.

Rebuilding after Cyclone Harold. UNICEF staff and members of the local community set up a tent to be used as a temporary clinic in the area damaged by Cyclone Harold at St. Henry South East Pentecost. (Photo by © UNICEF/UNI340915/Shing)

Appendix

	Disaster displacements	Share of total
East Asia	**75,874,000**	**33.7%**
People's Republic of China	70,439,000	31.3%
Japan	4,612,000	2.0%
Democratic People's Republic of Korea	565,000	0.3%
Taipei,China	176,000	0.1%
Republic of Korea	50,000	0.0%
Mongolia	17,000	0.0%
Macau, China	8,500	0.0%
Hong Kong, China	5,700	0.0%
Southeast Asia	**69,155,000**	**30.7%**
Philippines	49,312,000	21.9%
Indonesia	6,585,000	2.9%
Viet Nam	4,794,000	2.1%
Myanmar	3,752,000	1.7%
Thailand	2,919,000	1.3%
Malaysia	801,000	0.4%
Cambodia	761,000	0.3%
Lao People's Democratic Republic	207,000	0.1%
Timor-Leste	21,000	0.0%
Brunei Darussalam	150	0.0%
South Asia	**61,434,000**	**27.3%**
India	41,449,000	18.4%
Bangladesh	14,116,000	6.3%
Nepal	3,386,000	1.5%
Sri Lanka	2,460,000	1.1%
Bhutan	24,000	0.0%
Maldives	390	0.0%
Central and West Asia	**17,930,000**	**8.0%**
Pakistan	16,411,000	7.3%
Afghanistan	863,000	0.4%
Republic of Türkiye	381,000	0.2%
Kazakhstan	79,000	0.0%
Uzbekistan	70,000	0.0%
Azerbaijan	68,000	0.0%

	Disaster displacements	Share of total
Tajikistan	41,000	0.0%
Kyrgyz Republic	14,000	0.0%
Georgia	3,400	0.0%
The Pacific	**914,000**	**0.4%**
Australia	217,000	0.1%
Papua New Guinea	203,000	0.1%
Fiji	189,000	0.1%
Vanuatu	175,000	0.1%
Solomon Islands	26,000	0.0%
New Zealand	23,000	0.0%
Tonga	17,000	0.0%
Northern Mariana Islands	15,000	0.0%
Samoa	9,200	0.0%
Federated States of Micronesia	6,800	0.0%
New Caledonia	6,100	0.0%
Tuvalu	5,800	0.0%
American Samoa	5,000	0.0%
French Polynesia	4,700	0.0%
Palau	4,100	0.0%
Guam	2,900	0.0%
Kiribati	2,500	0.0%
Marshall Islands	1,400	0.0%
Cook Islands	670	0.0%

Endnotes

1 United Nations Office for the Coordination of Humanitarian Affairs (OCHA). 2017. Breaking the impasse. New York.

2 This timeframe has been selected on the basis of the quality and availability of data, as data before 2010 was not comprehensive enough.

3 This subregional breakdown corresponds to that of the Asian Development Bank.

4 IDMC. 2019. Global Report on Internal Displacement 2019.

5 UN-HABITAT. 2014. Pro-Poor Urban Climate Resilience in Asia and the Pacific: Quick Guide for Policymakers.

6 IDMC. 2017. Dam Displacement - Case Study Series.

7 ADB placed on hold its assistance in Myanmar effective 1 February 2021. ADB Statement on New Developments in Myanmar (published on 10 March 2021). No consultations or engagement took place after 31 January 2021.

8 IDMC. 2017. Dam Displacement - Case Study Series; Mekong River Commission for Sustainable Development. 2020. Understanding Mekong River's hydrological conditions.

9 IDMC. 2019. Flood Displacement Risk - An Urban Perspective.

10 Pui Man Kam et al. 2021. Global warming and population change both heighten future risk of human displacement due to river floods. IOP Science Journal. Environ. Res. Lett. 16 044026.

11 Relief Web. 2014. Asia Pacific Regional Hazard Map: Tectonic Plates and Faults.

12 Relief Web. 2014. Asia Pacific Regional Hazard Map: Tectonic Plates and Faults.

13 Y. Dou et al. 2018. Rapid Population Growth throughout Asia's Earthquake-Prone Areas: A Multiscale Analysis. International Journal of Environmental Research and Public Health. 15(9). p.p. 1893.

14 K. Goda et al. 2019. Cascading Geological Hazards and Risks of the 2018 Sulawesi Indonesia Earthquake and Sensitivity Analysis of Tsunami Inundation Simulations. Frontiers in Earth Science. 4 October.

15 Derived and computed from the EM-DAT database 2022.

16 A pyroclastic flow is a dense, fast-moving flow of solidified lava pieces, volcanic ash, and hot gases.

17 IDMC. 2018. Global Report on Internal Displacement (GRID). Indonesia and Vanuatu: Displacement for Good Reason.

18 Relief Web. 2021. Asia-Pacific Policy Brief – Recommendations on managing risk and addressing disaster displacement: challenges, effective practices and solutions.

19 IDMC. 2018. No matter of choice: displacement in a changing climate.

20 Date when drought-displacement data became available.

21 IDMC GRID. 2019. Afghanistan: Drought displaced as many as conflict.

22 IFRC. 2021. Afghanistan – Over 80% of country in serious drought.

23 OCHA. 2022. Afghanistan, ICCT Real-Time Response Overview.

24 C. Tronquet. 2015. From Vunidogoloa to Kenani: An Insight into Successful Relocation.

25 IDMC GRID. 2021. Internal Displacement in a Changing Climate.

26 World Bank Population Database (accessed 29 June 2022).

27 World Bank Indicators (accessed 29 June 2022).

28 R. Davies. 2013. Flooding in China[a], 2010. Floodlist. 31 March.

29 World Bank and GFDRR. 2020. Learning from Experience: Insights from China's Progress in Disaster Risk Management. Washington, DC.

30 World Bank. 2021. Nature-based solutions in China: Financing "sponge cities" for integrated urban flood management.

31 Global Times. 2021. Chinese experts refute BBC report claiming Zhengzhou floods broke sponge city myth. 23 July.

32 IDMC. 2022. Children and youth in internal displacement. p. 34.

33 Reduce Flooding blog. 2021. China's "Sponge Cities". 31 July.

34 Earth.org. 2021. Sponge City Concepts Could Be The Answer to China's Impending Water Crisis. 30 August; C. Zevenbergen et al. 2018. Transitioning to Sponge Cities: Challenges and Opportunities to Address Urban Water Problems in China. Water. 10 (9). 1230.

35 Y. Jiang et al. 2018. Urban pluvial flooding and stormwater management: A contemporary review of China's challenges and "sponge cities" strategy, Environmental Science & Policy. Volume 80. p.p. 132–143.

[a] ADB recognizes "China" as the People's Republic of China.

36 Asia Insurance Review. 2019. China: Typhoon Lekima spells US$10bn economic loss in August. 10 September.

37 United Nations, Economic and Social Commission for Asia and the Pacific (UNESCAP). 2020. The Disaster Riskscape across East and North-East Asia.

38 IDMC. 2017. Protracted disaster displacement: Japan Case Study.

39 IDMC GRID. 2021. Internal Displacement in a Changing Climate.

40 A dzud condition is characterised by deterioration of the weather conditions in winter and spring leading to shortage of pasture and water for livestock suffering massive die-off. By its intensity, dzud is categorised as a dzud situation and near-dzud situation. Source: United Nations Mongolia Country Team, 2016. UN Rapid Assessment Mission: Impact of Dzud Situation (1-6 February 2016).

41 The Economist. 2020. Mongolia's dealy winters are becoming more frequent. 10 February.

42 European Civil Protection and Humanitarian Aid Operations, 2022. Mongolia Factsheet (accessed 29 June2022).

43 Y. Hijioka et al. 2014. Climate Change 2014: Impacts, Adaptation, and Vulnerability. Part B: Regional Aspects. Contribution of Working Group II to the Fifth Assessment Report of the Intergovernmental Panel on Climate Change (IPCC). Cambridge University Press, Cambridge, UK and New York, NY. p.p. 1327–1370.

44 Norwegian Refugee Council (NRC) and IDMC. 2013. The risk of disaster-induced displacement in south-east Asia and China.

45 Government of the Philippines, Department of Social Welfare and Development (DSWD), IOM, IDMC, SAS. 2014. The Evolving Picture of Displacement in the Walk of Typhoon Haiyan. Manila.

46 Government of the Philippines. N.D. https://ndrrmc.gov.ph/attachments/article/2926/Y_It_Happened.pdfY It Happened. Manila.

47 OCHA, 2022. Philippines: Super Typhoon Rai (Odette) Humanitarian Needs and Priorities Revision (Dec 2021 - Jun 2022). 2 February.

48 OCHA, 2022. Philippines: Super Typhoon Rai (Odette) Humanitarian Needs and Priorities Revision (Dec 2021 - Jun 2022). 2 February.

49 Think Hazard. Vietnam Cyclone Report (accessed 20 June 2022).

50 UNESCAP. 2021. Asia-Pacific Disaster Report 2021.

51 UNESCAP. 2021. Asia-Pacific Disaster Report 2021.

52 UNDP, 2021. Household and Building Damage Assessment of Floods in Timor-Leste.

53 M. Oppenheimer et al. 2019. Sea Level Rise and Implications for Low-Lying Islands, Coasts and Communities. In: IPCC Special Report on the Ocean and Cryosphere in a Changing Climate. University Press, Cambridge, UK and New York, NY, USA, p.p. 321–445.

54 A. F. Medina. 2022. Indonesia Passes Bill to Build New Capital City: Deadline 2024. ASEAN Briefing. 25 January.

55 ADPC, UNDRR. 2020. Disaster Risk Reduction in Viet Nam: Status Report 2020 ; B. Eyler et al. N.D. https://www.stimson.org/2022/mdm-one-year-findings/Mekong Dam Monitor at One Year: What Have We Learned? (accessed 29 June 2022).

56 IDMC GRID. 2022. Spotlight – Myanmar: Disaster displacement, the other side of the crisis; IDMC. N.D. Philippines Country Profile (accessed 29 June 2022).

57 World Bank. Population, total – South Asia, World (accessed 21 April 2021); ADB. 2010. Climate Change in South Asia, Strong Responses for Building a Sustainable Future. Manila.

58 IDMC. 2015. The risk of disaster-induced displacement in South Asia; UN Bangladesh. 2020. HCTT Response Plan, Monsoon Floods, Coordinated Appeal, July 2020-March 2021. 4 August.

59 The Southwest monsoon, also called the summer monsoon, brings heavy rainfall from June to September. The Northwest monsoon, also known as the winter monsoon, occurs from October to February.

60 Government of India, Meteorological Department. 2020. New Normal Dates of Onset/Progress and Withdrawal of Southwest Monsoon over India. Delhi; Government of India, Meteorological Department. 2021. Statement on Climate of India during 2020. 5 January. Delhi.

61 SASCOF-19. 2021. Consensus Statement on the Seasonal Forecast over South Asia for the 2021 Southwest Monsoon Season. 10 June.

62 Government of India, Meteorological Department. 2021. Press Release – Salient Features of Monsoon 2021. 30 September; The Indian Express. 2022. South India records over 60% surplus rain during NE monsoon. 30 March.

63 T. Deshpande. 2021. Climate Change is Making India's Monsoon More Erratic. India Spend. 11 October; S. Clemens et al. 2021. Remote and local drivers of Pleistocene, South Asian summer monsoon precipitation: A test for future predictions. Science Advances. 7 (23), eabg3848.

64 Reports provided to IDMC by IOM for Khulna division.

65 B. Kirtman et al. 2013. Near-term Climate Change: Projections and Predictability. In: Climate Change 2013: The Physical Science Basis. Contribution of Working Group I to the Fifth Assessment Report of the Intergovernmental Panel on Climate Change; S. Sarkar. 2020. Cyclones rise as climate change heats up Indian Ocean. 5 June; National Geographic Database. Monsoon (accessed 21 April 2021).

66 S. Modak and Y. Jameel. 2021. https://www.orfonline.org/expert-speak/south-asias-tryst-with-floods/ South Asia's tryst with floods: A story less-known. Observer Researcher Foundation (ORF). 22 September.

67 D. Jarayam. 2020. https://climate-diplomacy.org/magazine/cooperation/south-asias-disaster-risk-reduction-policy-requires-overhaulSouth Asia's disaster risk reduction policy requires an overhaul. Climate Diplomacy. 14 October.

68 SEEDS and CRED. 2018. Decoding the monsoon floods. Delhi; M. S. G. Adnan et al. 2019. Have coastal embankments reduced flooding in Bangladesh? Sci Total Environ. 10 September. 10(682). p.p. 405-416.

69 M. S. G. Adnan et al. 2019. Have coastal embankments reduced flooding in Bangladesh? Sci Total Environ. 10 September. 682. p.p. 405–416; IFRC. 2018. Bangladesh: Displacement due to embankment collapse Emergency Plan of Action DREF n° MDRBD021. Z. H. Chowdhury. 2020. Bangladesh's hidden climate costs. The New Humanitarian. 9 December.

70 R. Bilham. 2014. Aggravated Earthquake Risk in South Asia: Engineering versus Human Nature. Science Direct. Hazards and Disasters Series. p.p. 103–141.

71 A. Witze. 2015. Mappers rush to pinpoint landslide risk in Nepal. Nature. 521. p.p.133–134 ; J. Qiu. 2016. Killer Landslides: The Lasting Legacy of Nepal's Quake. Scientific American. 25 April; N. Rosser et al. 2021. Changing significance of landslide Hazard and risk after the 2015 Mw 7.8 Gorkha, Nepal Earthquake. Science Direct. 10.100159.

72 S.V.R.K. Prabhakar et al. 2018. Transboundary Impacts of Climate Change in Asia: Making a Case for Regional Adaptation Planning and Cooperation. Hayama, Japan.

73 Bay of Bengal Initiative for Multi-Sectoral Technical and Economic Cooperation (BIMSTEC), 2022.. About Bimstec (accessed,29 June 2022); Coalition of Disaster Resilient Infrastructure, https://cdri.world/, (accessed, 29 June 2022).

74 I. Bubkenko eto al. 2020. Climate change in Central Asia, Illustrated Summary. Regional Environmental Centre for Central Asia.

75 ADB, World Bank. 2010. Pakistan Floods 2010: Preliminary Needs Assessment.

76 ADB and World Bank Group. 2021. Climate Risk Country Profile: Afghanistan (2021).

77 UN Spider. 2020. Dam Failure Uzbekistan: Satellite Based Observations. 19 May. IFRC. 2020. Kazakhstan – Floods – Emergency Plan of Action (EpoA) DREF Operation n° MDRKZ009. 14 May.

78 Cabar-Asia. 2020. Residents of Kazakh Flooded Villages Are Waiting for Reparations From Uzbekistan. 6 May; Floodlist. 2020. Uzbekistan and Kazakhstan – Thousands Evacuate After Dam Fails; Z. Shayakakhmetova. 3 May. The Astana Times. 2020. Kazakhstan and Uzbekistan Unitedly Deal With Flood Consequences After Major Dam Collapse In Region. 11 May.

79 IDMC, 2019. Afghanistan: Drought displaced as many as conflict. In: Global Report on Internal Displacement 2019.

80 ReliefWeb. N.D. Afghanistan: Drought – 2018-2019 (accessed 6 April 2020); IPC. 2019. Afghanistan, Acute Food Insecurity Analysis August 2019–March 2020. 30 September.

81 IFRC, Afghanistan. 2021. Over 80% of country in serious drought. 4 August.

82 OCHA, Afghanistan. 2022. ICCT Real-Time Response Overview. 11 January.

83 IDMC. 2022. Global Report on Internal Displacement 2022.

84 Foreign Affairs. 2016. Water Wars in Central Asia, 24 August; Water, Peace and Security. 2021. Conflicts over water and water infrastructure at the Tajik-Kyrgyz border: A looming threat for Central Asia?; FAO. 2017. Water report No. 44 – Drought characteristics and management in Central Asia and Turkey.

85 World Bank, 2021. Report –Groundswell Part 2: Acting on Internal Climate Migration

86 World Bank, 2021. Report –Groundswell Part 2: Acting on Internal Climate Migration

87 E. Gurenko et al. 2006. Earthquake Insurance in Turkey: History of the Turkish Catastrophe Insurance Pool. The World Bank: Washington D.C

88 Daily Sabah. 2021. Why is Turkey so prone to earthquakes? 4 June; Think Hazard. Turkey Earthquake Report (accessed 29 June 2022).

89 E. Damci et al. 2015. Damages and causes on the structures during the October 23, 2011 Van earthquake in Turkey. Science Direct. Case Studies in Construction Materials 3. p.p. 112–131.

90 IFRC. 2016. Afghanistan: Earthquake – DREF Final Report (MDRAF003).

91 IFRC. 2015. Pakistan: Earthquake 2015 - DREF Operation n° MDRPK012 - Emergency Plan of Action Final Report; Government of Pakistan (Khyber Pakhtunkhwa), Provincial Disaster Management Authority. 2015. Earthquake Recovery Plan. Islamabad.

92 IFRC. 2015. Pakistan: Earthquake 2015 - DREF Operation n° MDRPK012 - Emergency Plan of Action Final Report.

93 UNESCAP. 2020. The Disaster RiskscapeAcross North and Central Asia: Key Takeaways for Stakeholders.

94 World Bank. 2021. Report –Groundswell Part 2: Acting on Internal Climate Migration; IPCC. 2022. Climate Change 2022: Impacts, Adaptation and Vulnerability. Summary for Policy Makers.

95 UN Climate Change Conference (COP23). 2017/18. Kiribati Forecast; J. Shamoun et al. 2021. Climate Change and Forced Migration: A Focus on Kiribati.

96 Kindernothilfe et al. 2021. WorldRiskReport 2021 – Focus: Social Protection.

97 ADB. 2016.The Emergence of Pacific Urban Villages. Manila; M. Keen and J. Barber. 2016. Pacific urbanisation: changing times. DevPolicy Blog. 25 February.

98 Government of Australia, Bureau of Meteorology. South Pacific tropical cyclone season outlook (accessed 29 June 2022). Canberra.

99 IFRC. 2020. Pacific National Societies respond to Cyclone Harold in the time of COVID-19.; L. Cornish. 2020. First came the coronavirus. And then the cyclone hit. Devex. 21 May; E. Du Parc. 2020; COVID-19 and internal displacement in the Asia-Pacific: Towards local, rapid and inclusive disasters responses.

100 ReliefWeb. 2012. Papua New Guinea: Floods and Landslides – Jan 2012; IFRC. 2012. Papua New Guinea: Floods – Information Bulletin n° 1.

101 W. Cai et al. 2021. Opposite response of strong and moderate positive Indian Ocean Dipole to global warming. Nature Climate Change. 11. p.p. 27–32.

102 Government of Australia. 2020. Royal Commission into National Natural Disaster Arrangements. Canberra.

103 Australian Red Cross. 2020. Register. Find. Reunite Registration Data. Received by IDMC via email 17 March; Parliament of Australia. 2020. 2019–20 Australian bushfires—frequently asked questions: a quick guide. 12 March. Canberra; IDMC. 2020. The 2019-2020 Australian Bushfires: From Temporary Evacuation to Longer-Term Displacement.

104 W. Steffen and S. Bradshaw. 2021. Hitting Home: The Compounding Costs of Climate Inaction.

105 ICRC. 2018. Papua New Guinea: Earthquake Response Update.

106 As Papua New Guinea mainly dominates this trend, the proportion of the Pacific population living within 10km of the coast jumps to 97% when Papua New Guinea is excluded. N. L. Andrew et al. 2019. Coastal proximity of populations in 22 Pacific Island Countries and Territories. PloS ONE. 14(9): e0223249; IPCC. 2019. Chapter 4: Sea Level Rise and Implications for Low-Lying Islands, Coasts and Communities, Special Report on the Ocean and Cryosphere in a Changing Climate.

107 IPCC. 2022.Climate Change 2022: Impacts, Adaptation and Vulnerability. Summary for Policy Makers.

108 Government of Fiji. 2017. 5-Year and 20-Year National Development Plan. Suva; The Guardian. 2018. Island of no return: Vanuatu evacuates entire population of volcanic Ambae. April; Radio New Zealand. 2018. Vanuatu govt finalising 'second home' for Ambae residents. June; Government of Vanuatu. 2018. Progress made on Maewo second home for Ambae people. Port Vila; U. Rakova. N.D. Carterets Integrated Relocation Program.

109 U. Rakova. N.D. Carterets Integrated Relocation Program.

110 IOM. 2015. Assessing the Evidence: Migration, Environment and Climate Change in Papua New Guinea ; K. Fainu. 2021. An impossible choice: the Pacific's climate crisis. The Guardian. 16 October.

111 IOM. 2015. Assessing the Evidence: Migration, Environment and Climate Change in Papua New Guinea ; R. Bronen. 2014. Choice and necessity relocations in the Arctic and South Pacific. Forced Migration Review. Issue 45.

112 Government of Fiji, Ministry of Economy. 2018. Planned Relocation Guidelines. Suva; Government of Vanuatu. 2018. National Policy on Climate Change and Disaster-Induced Displacement. Port Vila; UN. 2021. Pacific Regional Consultation on Internal Displacement. Record of discussions; C. Farbotko et al. 2020. Relocation planning must address voluntary immobility. Nature Climate Change. 10. p.p. 702–704.

113 M. Yee et al. 2022. Climate Change, Voluntary Immobility, and Place-Belongingness: Insights from Togoru, Fiji. Climate 10.3 (2022): 46.

114 J. Bryant-Tokalau. 2018. Indigenous Pacific Approaches to Climate Change. ResearchGate; K. Morrison. 2017. The Role of Traditional Knowledge to Frame Understanding of Migration as Adaptation to the "Slow Disaster" of Sea Level Rise in the South Pacific. Springer, Cham.

115 UNESCAP considers two climate change scenarios using 'representative concentration pathways' (RCPs). The first is a moderate scenario where RCP is 4.5 and the second is the worst-case scenario where RCP is 8.5. Under RCP 4.5, these losses will increase to $1.1 trillion, and under RCP 8.5, to around $1.4 trillion.

116 UNESCAP. 2019. Asia-Pacific Disaster Report 2019.

117 UNESCAP. 2021. Resilience in a riskier world: Managing systemic risks from biological and other natural hazards Asia-Pacific Disaster Report 2021. UNESCAP includes natural and biological hazards in this estimate.

118 IDMC. 2021. Unveiling the cost of internal displacement. September.

119 OCHA. 2018. Central Sulawesi Earthquake Response Plan (Oct 2018 – Dec 2018). 4 October.

120 OCHA. 2018. Central Sulawesi Earthquake Response Plan (Oct 2018 – Dec 2018). 4 October.

121 IDMC. 2020. The 2019-2020 Australian Bushfires: From Temporary Evacuation to Longer-Term Displacement.

122 P. Maas et al. 2020. Using social media to measure demographic responses to natural disaster: Insights from a large-scale Facebook survey following the 2019 Australia Bushfires. Arvix.org. 2008.03665. 11 August.

123 Australian Red Cross. 2020. Australian Bushfires Report: 1 January –15 April 2020.

124 IDMC. 2020. The 2019-2020 Australian Bushfires: From Temporary Evacuation to Longer-Term Displacement.

125 Zhang, Hui, et.al. 2019. Bounce Forward: Economic Recovery in Post-Disaster Fukushima. Sustainability. 11(23). p.p. 6736.

126 IDMC GRID. 2022. Global Report on Internal Displacement 2022.

127 See OCHA. 2021, Humanitarian Response Plan: Afghanistan 2021 revision; OCHA. 2021. Humanitarian Response Plan: Myanmar, 2021.

128 ADB. 2019. Asian Development Outlook 2019: Strengthening disaster resilience. Manila.

129 IDMC. 2021. Sudden-Onset Hazards and the Risk of Future Displacement in Vanuatu.

130 UNESCAP. 2018. Disaster Resilience for Sustainable Development: Asia-Pacific Disaster Report 2017.

131 IDMC. 2021.Addressing internal displacement in the context of climate change.

132 UNESCAP. 2018. Disaster Resilience for Sustainable Development: Asia-Pacific Disaster Report 2017.

133 ADB. 2019. Asian Development Outlook (ADO) 2019: Strengthening Disaster Resilience. Manila.

134 IDMC GRID. 2022. Global Report on Internal Displacement 2022.

135 UNICEF and IDMC. 2019. Equitable access to quality education for internally displaced children .

136 P. Calvi-Parisetti. 2013. Older people and displacement. Forced Migration Review. 43.

137 HelpAge International. 2013a. Nutrition interventions for older people in emergencies.

138 HelpAge International. 2013b. Older people in emergencies: Identifying and reducing risks.

139 C. Watanabe et al. 2004. Journal of Traumatic Stress. 17 (1). pp. 63–67. https://doi.org/10.1023/b:-jots.0000014678.79875.30

140 IDMC. 2020. Women and girls in internal displacement.

141 Government of Fiji. 2016. Post-Disaster Needs Assessment—Tropical Cyclone Winston. Suva.

142 S. Fisher. 2010. Violence Against Women and Natural Disasters: Findings From Post-Tsunami Sri Lanka. Violence Against Women. 16(8). p.p. 902–918; N. Rezwana and R. Pain. 2021. Gender based violence before, during, and after cyclones: Slow violence and layered disasters. Disasters. 45(4). p.p. 741–761.

143 IDMC. Country Profile Nepal (accessed 29 June 2022).

144 IRC and USAID. 2021. Cycles of Displacement Understanding Exclusion, Discrimination and Violence Against LGBTQI People in Humanitarian Contexts; Gender in humanitarian action Asia and the Pacific Working Group. 2017. Integrating Gender into Humanitarian Action: Good Practices from Asia-Pacific 6.

145 The New Humanitarian. 2014. Lost in the chaos – LGBTI people in emergencies. 14 August.

146 D. Dominey-Howes et al. 2013. Queering disasters: on the need to account for LGBTI experiences in natural disaster contexts. Gender, Place & Culture: A Journal of Feminist Geography. 21(7). p.p. 905-918, DOI: 10.1080/0966369X.2013.802673. HPN. 2008. Aravanis: voiceless victims of the tsunami. December.

147 S. Ritholtz. 2020. LGBTQ+ people left out by exclusionary Covid-19 aid practices. The New Humanitarian. 24 June.

148 J. C. Gaillard et al. 2016. Beyond men and women: a critical perspective on gender and disaster. Disasters. 22 September.

149 UNESCAP. 2019. Disability at a Glance 2019: Investing in Accessibility in Asia and the Pacific.

150 UNHCR, IDMC, IDA. 2021. Disability, Displacement and Climate Change.; F. Smith et al. 2017. Disability and Climate Resilience A Literature Review.

151 CBM. 2020. Cyclone Amphan: Inclusive Rapid Needs Assessment – Bangladesh: Satkhira, Patuakhali and Bagerhat Districts.

152 IDMC. 2021. Disabilities, disasters and displacement.

153 Australasian College for Emergency Medicine. 2020. Submission to the Royal Commission into Violence, Abuse, Neglect and Exploitation of People with Disability. Lismore.

154 Australasian College for Emergency Medicine. 2020. Submission to the Royal Commission into Violence, Abuse, Neglect and Exploitation of People with Disability. Lismore.

155 United Nations General Assembly (UNGA). 2017. Report of the Special Rapporteur on the rights of indigenous peoples. 1 November.

156 UNGA. 2019. Indigenous people's rights in the context of borders, migration and displacement. 18 September.

157 The International Work Group for Indigenous Affairs (IWGIA). 2021. The Indigenous World 2021.

158 S. Lambert and J. Scott. 2019. International disaster risk reduction strategies and Indigenous Peoples. The International Indigenous Policy Journal. 10(2).

159 UNDRR. 2019. Disaster displacement: How to reduce risks, address impacts and strengthen resilience.

160 IDMC. 2020. Internal displacement 2020: Mid-year update.

161 T. Hadi. et.al. 2021. Seeking Shelter: The factors that influence refuge since Cyclone Gorky in the Coastal Area of Bangladesh. Progress in Disaster Science. 11. October.

162 Based on an extrapolation from a survey conducted by the Prefectural University of Hiroshima on the needs of evacuees and issues related to shelter management in Hiroshima, Okayama and Ehime following Typhoon Jongdari, only 400 out of the 10,000 people surveyed were considered evacuees. The Japan Times Online. 2018. "Only 3.6 percent of Hiroshima residents had evacuated when July rain disaster struck". August 3.

163 IDMC GRID. 2019. Spotlight Japan.

164 J. Bateman and B. Edwards. 2002. Gender and Evacuation: A Closer Look at Why Women Are More Likely to Evacuate for Hurricanes. Natural Hazards Review. 3(3). p.p. 1527–6988.

165 IDMC. 2020. The 2019-2020 Australian Bushfires: From Temporary Evacuation to Longer-Term Displacement.

166 P. Maas et al. 2020. Using social media to measure demographic responses to natural disaster: Insights from a large-scale Facebook survey following the 2019 Australia Bushfires. Arvix.org. 2008.03665. 11 August.

167 IDMC, 2020. Global Report on Internal Displacement. Spotlight: the Philippines.

168 Nepal Earthquake Housing Reconstruction Multi-Donor Fund, 2021. Annual Report July 2020 - June -2021.

169 E. Bower and S. Weerasinghe. 2021. Leaving Place, Restoring Home: Enhancing the evidence base on planned relocation cases in the context of hazards, disasters, and climate change.

170 M. Koch-Weser and S. Guggenheim, ed. 2021. Social Development in the World Bank: Essays in Honor of Michael M. Cernea. Cham, Switzerland: Springer Nature Switzerland.

171 E. Correa et al. 2011. Populations at Risk of Disaster: A Resettlement Guide. World Bank: Washington D.C.

172 AHA Centre. 2021. The ASEAN Village: A Tangible Support and Solidarity from ASEAN and Partners for the Community in Palu City.

173 Government of Viet Nam, Disaster Management Authority. Website in Vietnamese (accessed 30 June 2022). Hanoi.

174 IFRC and RCRC. 2021. Responding to Disasters and Displacement in a Changing Climate.

175 Inter-Agency Standing Committee. 2010. Durable Solutions for Internally Displaced Persons.

176 IPCC. 2022. Climate Change 2022: Impacts, Adaptation and Vulnerability. Summary for Policymakers.

177 V. Clement et al. 2021. Groundswell Part 2: Acting on Internal Climate Migration. Washington, D.C.: World Bank.

178 IPCC. Regional Fact Sheet: Asia (accessed 30 June 2022).

179 Government of the United States, NASA. Global Temperature Database (accessed 30 June 2022). Washington D.C.

180 IPCC. 2022. Climate Change 2022: Impacts, Adaptation and Vulnerability. Summary for Policy Makers.

181 WMO. 2021. Press Release: State of Climate in 2021: Extreme events and major impacts; Government of the United States, National Oceanic and Atmospheric Administration (NOAA). 2020. Annual 2020 Global Climate Report. Washington.

182 IDMC GRID. 2019. Flood Displacement Risk - An urban perspective.

183 World Bank. 2015. IBRD, Flood Risk Management in Dhaka: A Case for Eco-Engineering Approaches and Institutional Reform.

184 IDMC. 2021. Sudden-Onset Hazards and the Risk of Future Displacement in Vanuatu

185 N. Diffenbaugh. 2020. Verification of extreme event attribution: Using out-of-sample observations to assess changes in probabilities of unprecedented events. Science Advances. 6(12).

186 WMO. N.D. United in Science 2021 (accessed 30 June 2022).

187 UNDRR. 2015. Sendai Framework for Disaster Risk Reduction 2015-2030.

188 UNDRR. 2015. Sendai Framework for Disaster Risk Reduction 2015-2030.

189 UNDRR. 2018. Technical guidance for monitoring and reporting on progress in achieving the global targets of the Sendai Framework for disaster risk reduction.

190 UNDRR. 2020. Sendai Framework Monitoring in Europe and Central Asia: A Regional Snapshot.

191 IOM and IDMC. 2022. Developing indicators on displacement for Disaster Risk Reduction.

192 Partial data means the country only reports on this indicator for some disaster events, or in some parts of the country, often on an ad-hoc basis.

193 IDMC. 2021. Internal Displacement Index 2021.

194 IDMC. 2021. Internal Displacement Index 2021.

195 Regional Consultative Committee on Disaster Management, 2022. Website (accessed 30 June 2022)

196 Vanuatu National Disaster Management Office and IOM. 2020. Vanuatu Displacement Tracking Report - Tropical Cyclone Harold.

197 Vanuatu National Disaster Management Office and IOM. 2020. Vanuatu Displacement Tracking Report - Tropical Cyclone Harold.

198 IDMC and Inclusive Data Charter. 2021. Case Study: Steps taken by the Internal Displacement Monitoring Centre to understand the context for preparing its intersectional approach to data.

199 UNDRR. 2019. Disaster displacement: How to reduce risk, address impacts and strengthen resilience.

200 The IDI policy indicator is calculated as an unweighted average of the five sub-indicators mentioned. The acknowledgement of internal displacement in a policy is scored as 1 (yes) or 0 (no). The remaining indicators are allocated 0.5 points each for the inclusion of disaster displacement.

201 Government of the Philippines. 2020. National Disaster Risk Management Plan (2020-2030). Manila.

202 Government of the Philippines. 2011. National Climate Change Action Plan (NCCAP) 2011-2028. Manila.

203 Government of Bangladesh, Ministry of Disaster Management and Relief. 2017. National Plan for Disaster Management (2016-2020). Dhaka

204 Government of Bangladesh National Plan for Disaster Management (2016-2020). Dhaka.

205 Government of Bangladesh, Ministry of Disaster Management and Relief. 2020. National Plan for Disaster Management (2021-2025). Dhaka.

206 Government of Bangladesh, Ministry of Disaster Management and Relief. 2015. National strategy on the management of disaster and climate induced internal displacement. Dhaka.

207 Government of Bangladesh, Ministry of Disaster Management and Relief. 2015. National strategy on the management of disaster and climate induced internal displacement. Dhaka.

208 Government of India, National Disaster Management Authority. 2019. National Disaster Management Plan (NDMP). Delhi.

209 Government of Pakistan. 2012. National Climate Change Policy. Islamabad.

210 Government of Fiji. 2018. National Climate Change Policy 2018-2030. Suva. Government of Fiji. 2018. National Adaptation Plan: A pathway towards climate resilience. Suva.

211 Government of Fiji. 2018. Planned Relocation Guidelines - A framework to undertake climate change related relocation. Suva.

212 Government of New Zealand. 2019. National Disaster Resilience Strategy. Wellington; Government of Papua New Guinea, National Disaster Centre. 2017. National Disaster Risk Reduction Framework 2017-2030. Port Moresby; Government of Fiji. 2018. National Disaster Risk Reduction Policy 2018-2030. Suva.

213 IDMC. 2021. Viet Nam is a role model for responding to climate change displacement, but there are still lessons to be learned; IOM. 2017. IOM, Planning relocation in the context of environmental change in Hoa Binh Province, Northern Viet NamPlanning relocation in the context of environmental change in Hoa Binh Province, Northern Viet Nam.

214 IDMC. 2021. Viet Nam is a role model for responding to climate change displacement, but there are still lessons to be learned; UN Research Institute for Social Development (UNRISD). 2020. Transformative Adaptation to Climate Change and Informal Settlements in Coastal Cities: Entry Points for Jakarta and Ho Chi Minh City.

www.ingramcontent.com/pod-product-compliance
Lightning Source LLC
Chambersburg PA
CBHW051307270326
41926CB00030B/4762

* 9 7 8 9 2 9 2 6 9 7 2 8 0 *